Disney

ALICE in WONDERLAND

THE OFFICIAL COOKBOOK

MORE THAN 50 TOPSY-TURVY RECIPES
INSPIRED BY ALICE, THE MAD HATTER, AND MORE!

RECIPES BY ELENA P. CRAIG
TEXT BY S. T. BENDE
FOREWORD BY ASHLEY ECKSTEIN

INSIGHT EDITIONS

SAN RAFAEL · LOS ANGELES · LONDON

CONTENTS

Foreword 7
Introduction 9

CHAPTER ONE:
London

Lazy Daisies Garden Quiche 13
Fairy Cake Butterflies 15
Curiously Cornish Pasties 17
The Cat's Meow Milkshake 19
Fanciful Fish and Chips 20
Perfect Pistachio Stuffed Chicken 22
Savory Sausage Rolls 23
Perfectly Potted Cheese 25

CHAPTER TWO:
Down the Rabbit Hole

Curiouser and Curiouser Chocolate-Covered Digestive Cookies 29
Growth Potion 31
Magic Cook-keys 32
White Rabbit Graham Cracker Cottages 35
"I'm Really in a Stew" 37
Bill the Lizard's Ladder Bread 39
White Rabbit's Garden Crudité 41

CHAPTER THREE:
Ocean of Tears

An Ocean of Tears Blue Drink 45
Of Cabbage Rolls and Kings 46
The Sailor's Life Boat Crudité 49
"Whether Pigs Have Wings" Pastries 51
Caucus Race Ravioli 52
Sun and Moon Pizza Pie 55

CHAPTER FOUR:
Tulgey Wood

Tweedledee & Tweedledum Brownie Cake Pops   59
Garden Thistle Artichoke Dip   61
Cheshire Cat Panna Cotta   63
Golden Afternoon Greens   65
Fanciful Fruit Shrubs   67
"I'm Late!" Quick Roast Vegetables   68
White Rabbit's Quick Change Oats   69
Pocket Watch Cupcakes   71
Caterpillar Crostini   72
Moroccan Chicken and Olives   73
A-E-I-O Soup   75
Mushroom Perch Pie   76
Tulgey Wood Forest Cake   79
Forest Chutney   81
Crocodile Golden Scale Beets   83
Bread and Butterfly Toast   84
Who's Got the Rice Crispy Buttons?   87

CHAPTER FIVE:
A Mad Tea Party

He Went That Way Tea Sandwiches   93
Curiosi-tea   96
Teacup Treasures with Shrimp Salad   97
Dormouse Macarons   100
Pocket Watch Poppyseed Scones with Mock Clotted Cream   103
"I'm in a Jam" Homemade Strawberry-Lemon Jam   105
Unbirthday Par-tea Cupcakes   107

CHAPTER SIX:
The Red Queen's Kingdom

Toast Soldiers with Coddled Eggs   113
Painting the Roses Red Pavlova   115
Her Royal Majesty's Crown Roast   116
The Queen's Way Spiced Cider   117
Playing Card Strata   119
Oh, My Fur and Whiskers Skewers   120
Bittersweet Truffles   121
Very Good Advice Gummies   123
Queen of Hearts Tomato Tart   124

Glossary   126
Dietary Considerations   127

FOREWORD

"Sometimes, I believe as many as six *impossible things* before breakfast."

—Alice

This is my favorite quote from the Disney film *Alice in Wonderland*. I have it on a plaque in my kitchen and it's like a to-do list for my day. I must believe six impossible things before breakfast, just like I must take my vitamins and wash the dishes. As a life-long *Alice in Wonderland* fan, I've always associated my favorite story with food. With constant reminders throughout the book and movie to always make time for a snack whether it be a cookie to make you smaller or a potion to make you taller, my path always points me "This Way" to the kitchen. It's also because of *Alice in Wonderland* that I love tea parties. I delight over tea sandwiches and scones, cakes and pastries, and, of course, tea! That's why I was so excited and honored to write this foreword—a cookbook pairs with *Alice in Wonderland* just like Tweedledee belongs with Tweedledum.

However, if I could give you some very good advice as you try these recipes, make sure to always add a pinch of nonsense! Curiosity belongs in the kitchen, and when you are cooking or baking, you are in a world of your own. In my kitchen, I like to say, "My world, my rules." Just explore and experiment because what it is, it isn't, and what it shouldn't be, it should!

Finally, the secret ingredient in every recipe is your belief in the impossible. As you prepare each dish, it's important to believe in impossible things. Add a line to each recipe to believe at least one impossible thing while you are cooking or baking! The repetitive act of believing in the impossible will soon make the impossible possible and *that* is the best recipe of them all!

—Ashley Eckstein

INTRODUCTION

The whimsical world of Wonderland has captured countless hearts since our curious friend Alice first tumbled down the rabbit hole. Alice's adventures inspire dreamers, explorers, and creators alike, reminding us of the joy that can come from embracing the unknown. In a world where nothing is impossible and "most everyone's just a little bit mad," Alice's experiences highlight the magic within the unexpected and illuminate the unique beauty that can exist within any topsy-turvy world.

But Wonderland is not without its perils: As Alice quickly discovers, curiosity often leads to trouble! Luckily, Alice's extraordinary acquaintances are only too happy to nudge her along on her journey—and introduce her to the unique culinary treats that Wonderland has to offer. From Growth Potion to Unbirthday Par-tea Cupcakes, these delicious delicacies are every bit as fantastical as Alice's immeasurable imagination. Some of the recipes within these pages are delightfully outlandish, while others offer an enchanting spin on familiar treats. A-E-I-O-Soup is sure to delight young gastronomes, while the White Rabbit Graham Cracker Cottages offer an epicurean adventure that the White Rabbit would have found *most* useful when a certain young adventurer grew to an unexpected size right inside his home! Moroccan Chicken and Olives blends tantalizing spices, and fanciful Fairy Cake Butterflies are the perfect complement to an afternoon spent reading in the garden—provided that one's book contains pictures, of course (and don't worry—*ours* certainly does).

We're so very pleased that you've decided to join us on this indulgent adventure. We'll journey from foggy London Town to its neighboring sun-dappled villages, dive down the rabbit hole, sail through an ocean of tears, and weave our way through the ever-changing forests of Wonderland. After refreshments at a most peculiar tea party, we'll travel to the Royal Court to sample the delicacies favored by the Queen of Hearts. It's a most ambitious undertaking, so we *do* hope you've brought your appetite. After all, to believe as many as six impossible things before breakfast, one simply *must* have a proper selection of treats to enjoy afterward.

Ta-ta!

CHAPTER ONE

London

On the outskirts of foggy London Town, a white-steepled church sits beside a flower-filled meadow. This charming hamlet serves as the starting point for a most extraordinary gastronomic tour. The residents of Alice's village serve up a series of English delights, each of which reflects the culture of a nation steeped in duty and tradition. From a light morning quiche to quintessential British sausage rolls, our journey begins in the land of kings and queens. Here, even a Mad Hatter can keep calm and carry on . . . accompanied by a basket of fish and chips, of course!

Lazy Daisies Garden Quiche

 Yield: 6 to 8 servings **Vegetarian**

There's no finer way to prepare for the morning's lessons than with a light garden quiche. This savory tart offers a hearty blend of eggs and cheese—the perfect meal to kick off a day spent studying geography, history, and literature . . . or simply learning lots of things from the flowers.

Pie Crust:

2½ cups all-purpose flour
1 tablespoon poppy seeds, divided
1 teaspoon kosher salt
½ cup unsalted butter, very cold
¼ cup solid vegetable shortening, very cold
⅓ cup ice water
1 egg
Warm spices, such as paprika, turmeric, or curry, for painting

Filling:

1 bunch asparagus, roasted (see note)
1 bunch chives
4 large eggs
1 cup milk
1 cup heavy cream
½ teaspoon salt
Freshly ground black pepper
1 cup (about 2 ounces) grated Gruyère cheese

Special Tools:

Deep 9-inch pie pan
Small cookie cutters of flowers, butterflies, bees, and/or leaves

To make the pie crust: In a large bowl, combine the flour, 2 teaspoons of the poppy seeds, and the kosher salt. Cut the cold butter and the shortening into small pieces. Using a pastry cutter or two forks, work the butter and shortening into the flour mixture until all the pieces are pea size or smaller.

Add the ice water a little bit at a time, and use the pastry cutter to bring the dough together. As the dough starts to come together, switch to your hands or a spatula, starting with ⅓ cup ice water and using up to ½ cup ice water, until the dough just comes together.

Split the dough in half, turn out onto a floured surface, and roll out into a circle about ⅛ inch thick that extends a bit past the rim of your pie pan. Create a pleated edge. Refrigerate for 30 minutes.

Preheat the oven to 400°F. Roll out the second half of the dough, and use the cookie cutters to cut out shapes for decorating and serving.

Create an egg wash by whisking the egg with 1 tablespoon water. Brush the egg wash on all the pastry shapes, and use the remaining poppy seeds and spices to decorate. Chill for at least 15 minutes before baking in the oven for 7 to 9 minutes or until golden brown. Allow the shapes to cool completely, and store in an airtight container until serving.

Remove the pie pan from the refrigerator, and line it with two pieces of foil that extend over the sides. Fill the center of the pie pan with pie weights or dried beans, to keep the crust from puffing up. Bake for 20 minutes. Remove the pie pan from the oven, and remove the foil and pie weights; prick the bottom and sides with a fork, brush the crust with the egg wash, and return the pie pan to the oven. Bake for an additional 5 to 7 minutes or until the crust is a light golden brown. While the crust is baking, prepare the filling.

Continued on page 14

Continued from page 13

> ❋ **Notes:** To roast the asparagus, snap off the tough ends of each stalk, and toss the spears with a tablespoon of olive oil and a pinch of salt. Roast at 400°F for 5 to 7 minutes or until the spears are just fork tender. Allow the asparagus to cool before adding it to the quiche.
>
> Use kitchen shears to snip the chives. Chives bruise easily, so unless you're highly skilled with a kitchen knife, we highly recommend using kitchen shears to snip the chives into tiny bits.

To make the filling: Save a few pretty asparagus stalks for decoration, if desired. Cut the rest of the roasted asparagus into bite-size pieces, and set them aside.

Save several stems of the chives for decoration; snip the rest until you have 2 tablespoons.

In a large bowl, whisk the eggs until the mixture is homogeneous; then add the snipped chives, milk, cream, salt, and black pepper (to taste). Whisk again to combine.

When the pie crust is removed from the oven the second time, scatter the cheese over the bottom, followed by the asparagus pieces. Then pour the egg-and-milk mixture over the top.

Reduce the oven temperature to 375°F, and bake for 35 to 40 minutes until the filling is beginning to brown and the center of the filling jiggles only slightly. If the crust is becoming too brown, cover it with foil.

Allow the quiche to cool at least 15 minutes before decorating and serving. Quiche can be served warm, room temperature, or chilled. When the quiche has cooled completely, it should be refrigerated until you are ready to serve it. Quiche can be made a day ahead but should be decorated right before serving.

To decorate the quiche, use the extra asparagus, chive stems, and pastry shapes to create a garden scene. Additional pastry shapes can be used to decorate the serving dish or can be put in a bowl for snacking.

FAIRY CAKE BUTTERFLIES

 Yield: About 12 cakes **Vegetarian**

These tantalizing Fairy Cake Butterflies are inspired by Alice's daydreams, which are every bit as fantastical as the forest of Wonderland. With hints of rose and dollops of orange marmalade and raspberry jam, Fairy Cake Butterflies are a lovely dessert for any golden afternoon.

1 cup superfine sugar, plus 2 tablespoons for the muffin cups

1¼ cups all-purpose flour, plus 2 tablespoons more for the muffin cups

¾ cup salted butter, at room temperature, plus more for the muffin cups

3 eggs

1 teaspoon baking powder

3 to 5 drops red food coloring

3 to 5 drops yellow food coloring

¼ teaspoon pure rose extract

¼ teaspoon pure orange extract

⅔ cup heavy cream

About 6 teaspoons raspberry jam

About 6 teaspoons orange marmalade

Powdered sugar, for garnish

Preheat the oven to 350°F. Mix together 2 tablespoons of the superfine sugar and 2 tablespoons of flour in a small bowl. Butter twelve standard muffin cups; then dust with the flour/sugar mixture, tapping out the excess.

In a large bowl, using a handheld mixer on medium speed or a wooden spoon, cream together the butter and the remaining sugar until smooth and creamy. Add the eggs, one at a time, together with a spoonful of the flour with the first egg, to stop the mix from curdling; mix well after each addition. Fold in the remaining flour and the baking powder, mixing thoroughly.

Divide the mixture into two equal portions, and put each portion into a separate bowl. Color one portion with the red food coloring, and color the other portion with the yellow food coloring. Stir the rose extract into the red portion, and stir the orange extract into the yellow portion. Divide the mixtures evenly among the muffin cups, filling six cups with each color.

Bake until a cake tester comes out clean, 16 to 18 minutes. Let the muffins cool in the pan on a wire rack for 10 minutes; then turn out the cakes onto the rack, turn them upright, and let them cool completely.

Using a paring knife, slice a thin piece off the top of each cupcake; set aside.

Whip the cream with a handheld mixer on medium-high speed until stiff peaks form. Transfer the whipped cream to a piping bag fitted with a star tip, and pipe a dollop of cream onto the center of each cake.

Cut each removed top in half, and push each half into the whipped cream, to create wings.

Dust the cakes with powdered sugar. Place a scant teaspoon of raspberry jam down the center of the red set of wings, and place a scant teaspoon of marmalade down the center of each orange set of wings. Serve immediately.

CURIOUSLY CORNISH PASTIES

Yield: About 12 pasties

If one intends to spend one's day frolicking through the flowers, then convenience foods are an absolute must. These Cornish pasties provide the perfect transportable treat. Pork, apples, and a treasure trove of flavors are neatly constrained within the boundaries of this tidy, side-crimped pastry. Whether for tiptoeing through tulips or sitting for lessons, this recipe provides a hearty picnic snack that can easily be eaten on the go.

Pastry:

4½ cups all-purpose flour, plus more for the work surface

1¼ teaspoons kosher salt

1 cup (2 sticks) salted butter, very cold

1 cup plus 2 tablespoons cold water

Filling:

2 small apples, such as Granny Smith, peeled, halved, cored, and cut into ½-inch cubes

½ pound boneless pork shoulder (or boneless pork chop), trimmed of excess fat and cut into ½-inch cubes

¼ pound uncooked bacon, minced

1 tablespoon Worcestershire sauce

1 teaspoon dried sage (or 1 tablespoon minced fresh sage)

Salt and black pepper

To make the pastry: In a large bowl, combine the flour and kosher salt. Cut in the butter with a pastry cutter or two forks until the mixture resembles coarse crumbs. Mix in the water a bit at a time until the dough can be formed into a ball. Divide the dough in half, and pat each half into a disk. Wrap each disk in parchment, and refrigerate while you make the filling.

To make the filling: Combine the apples, pork, bacon, Worcestershire sauce, and sage in a large bowl; season with salt and black pepper, to taste, and mix well.

Preheat the oven to 375°F. Line two rimmed baking sheets with parchment paper. Generously flour a work surface. Roll out one dough disk about ⅛ inch thick. Using a saucer as a guide, cut out six circles, each about 6 inches in diameter (if needed, gather the scraps and reroll until you have six circles).

Divide half of the filling evenly among the circles, spooning it onto half of each circle and leaving ½ inch uncovered around the edge. Dampen the edge of each circle with water, fold the circles in half, and press down on the edge to seal. Crimp the edges with a fork or with your fingers. Prick the tops several times with a fork, to vent, and arrange the half-circles on one of the prepared baking sheets. Repeat with the remaining pastry and filling.

Bake the half-circles until they are barely golden on top and a thermometer inserted into the center of a pastry registers 165°F, about 20 minutes.

Serve the pasties warm or at room temperature with Forest Chutney (page 81) or Homemade Mustard (page 46). Pasties can be stored in an airtight container for 1 to 2 days. They can be reheated in a 350°F oven for about 10 minutes.

THE CAT'S MEOW MILKSHAKE

 Yield: 2 milkshakes **Vegetarian**

Alice's faithful friend Dinah knows a thing or two about fun. This curious kitten chases butterflies and flower petals across the sun-dappled meadow as she carefully explores every inch of her world. With her rose-tinted bow and cerulean eyes, Dinah would be tickled pink to see her favorite hues reflected in this blue-layered, strawberry-dusted, rich and creamy confection.

½ cup freeze-dried strawberries, divided

1 cup milk, divided

¼ cup butterfly pea flowers

2 tablespoons malted milk powder

½ cup heavy whipping cream

2 tablespoons powdered sugar

4 scoops vanilla ice cream, divided

Two small containers that can be sealed, such as mason jars

Place about ¼ cup of the freeze-dried strawberries in a sealable plastic bag. Using a meat tenderizer or rolling pin, pound them until most of the pieces turn to a fine dust.

In one of the containers, add ½ cup of the milk, about 2 tablespoons of the strawberry dust (reserve the rest for garnish), and the remaining ¼ cup of the strawberry pieces. Seal and shake vigorously to combine. In the second container, combine the remaining ½ cup of milk with the butterfly pea flowers; then seal the bag and shake. Refrigerate both containers for 1 hour.

After 1 hour, strain the butterfly pea mixture, squeezing the flowers dry and discarding them. Add the malted milk powder, and shake vigorously to combine. Keep the mixture refrigerated until it is needed.

When you are ready to serve the milkshakes, prepare the whipped cream by adding the cream and powdered sugar to a whipped cream canister or a large bowl and then beating on high until stiff peaks form. Set aside.

In a blender, combine the strawberry milk and two scoops of ice cream, and blend until smooth but still thick. Split the mixture between two tall glasses. In a clean blender pitcher, add the blue malted milk and the remaining two scoops of ice cream. Blend until smooth but still thick. Split this second mixture between the two glasses, layering it on top of the strawberry mixture.

Top the milkshakes with whipped cream and a sprinkle of reserved crushed strawberry.

Serve with straws or long spoons.

FANCIFUL FISH AND CHIPS

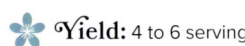 **Yield:** 4 to 6 servings

This traditional English meal pairs a well-known "brain food" with its crispy, fried counterpart. Fish and chips dates back to the early days of London Town, with the first chippy shop opening right around the time a certain White Rabbit scampered down his rabbit hole. What a curious coincidence!

Potatoes:

4 russet potatoes (about 3 pounds)
2 teaspoons salt, divided
4 tablespoons olive oil, for coating
2 teaspoons garlic powder
2 teaspoons onion powder
1 teaspoon smoked paprika
½ teaspoon dried dill
Zest of 1 lemon

Sauce:

⅓ cup mayonnaise
⅓ cup Greek yogurt
2 tablespoons malt vinegar
1 clove garlic, minced
1 tablespoon minced parsley

Fish:

1½ pounds cod or other whitefish
About 2 quarts oil (such as canola or peanut), for frying
1¼ cups all-purpose flour, divided
¼ cup mochi flour or rice flour
½ teaspoon baking powder
½ teaspoon paprika
½ teaspoon salt
½ teaspoon onion powder
1 to 1½ cups medium ale
Lemon wedges, for serving

To make the potatoes: Preheat the oven to 425°F, and line a baking sheet with parchment paper. Slice the potatoes in half lengthwise, and then slice them into thick wedges, about ¼ inch thick. Soak the slices for at least 25 minutes in cold water with 1 teaspoon of the salt added.

Dry off and lightly coat the potatoes in the olive oil, and place them on the prepared baking sheet. Bake for 30 to 45 minutes.

While the potatoes are baking, in a small bowl, combine the remaining teaspoon of salt with the garlic powder, onion powder, smoked paprika, dried dill, and lemon zest. As soon as the potatoes are done, remove them from the oven and sprinkle generously with the spice mixture.

To make the sauce: In a medium bowl, stir together the mayonnaise, Greek yogurt, malt vinegar, garlic, and parsley. Refrigerate the sauce until needed.

To make the fish: Slice the cod into 2- to 3-inch chunks, and set aside.

In a deep fryer or large Dutch oven, over medium-high heat, bring the oil up to 365°F (see the accompanying cautions on fry safety).

While the oil is heating, in a large bowl, combine ¾ cup of the all-purpose flour with the mochi flour, baking powder, paprika, salt, and onion powder. Set aside. Set up a low, shallow dish with the remaining ½ cup all-purpose flour for dredging. When the oil reaches 365°F, slowly add the beer to the flour mixture, whisking, until the batter is a bit thinner than pancake batter.

Working with one or two fish pieces at a time, dredge the fish in flour and then coat the pieces in batter. Fry for 2 to 4 minutes or until golden brown.

For garnish and serving, sprinkle the fish with additional minced parsley, lemon wedges, and sauce on the side, and add the potato slices.

Fry Station and Safety: If you're making something that requires deep frying, here are some important tips to keep you safe:

- If you don't have a dedicated deep fryer, use a Dutch oven or a high-walled sauté pan.
- Never have too much oil in the pan! You don't want hot oil spilling out as soon as you put the food in.
- Use only a suitable cooking oil, such as canola, peanut, or vegetable oil.
- Always keep track of the oil temperature with a thermometer; 350° to 375°F should do the trick.
- Never put too much food in the pan at the same time!
- Never put wet food in the pan. It will splatter and can cause burns.
- Always have a lid nearby to cover the pan, in case it starts to spill over or catch fire. A properly rated fire extinguisher is also great to have on hand, in case of emergencies.
- Never leave the pan unattended, and never let children near the pan.
- Never, ever put your face, your hand, or any other body part in the hot oil.

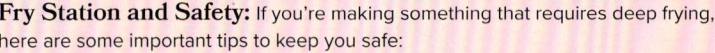

PERFECT PISTACHIO STUFFED CHICKEN

 Yield: 6 servings   **Gluten Free**

This nutty twist on a suppertime classic is a staple in many British households. Tart apples pair with sage and coriander to create a surprisingly unexpected blend that's sure to command the attention of even the most distractable diner. And as Alice whiles away the hours in a world of her own, this chicken will be soaking up the flavors of pistachio, almond, and pork. This protein-packed meal is guaranteed to give dreamers of all ages the energy they need to embark on their next grand adventure. Cheerio!

8 tablespoons salted butter, divided

½ pound ground pork

1 cup raw pistachios, roughly chopped

¼ cup ground almonds

½ tart apple, such as Granny Smith, finely chopped

2 tablespoons chopped sage leaves (about 2 stalks)

1 teaspoon ground coriander

½ teaspoon allspice

1 teaspoon salt

Freshly ground black pepper

Zest and juice of 1 lemon

1 whole chicken (4 to 6 pounds)

½ cup stock (chicken or vegetable)

In a large sauté pan over medium-high heat, melt 4 tablespoons of the butter. Add the pork, pistachios, almonds, apples, sage, coriander, allspice, salt, black pepper (to taste), and lemon zest. Sauté until the pork is cooked through, about 5 to 7 minutes. Set aside to cool.

Place the chicken in a shallow roasting pan, pat dry, and set aside. Preheat the oven to 400°F.

When the stuffing is cool enough to handle, loosely pack both cavities of the chicken, and close with toothpicks or lacers and twine. Rub the additional 4 tablespoons of butter under the breast skin, being careful not to tear the skin, and over the remainder of the bird. Pour the stock and the juice of the lemon into the bottom of the pan. Reserve any leftover stuffing for serving.

Roast for about 1½ hours or until the stuffing temperature reaches 165°F. Baste with the pan juices, and rotate every half-hour. Note that the temperature will rise up to an additional 5°F while resting.

When the chicken is done, remove it to a platter, tent with foil, and allow it to rest for 20 minutes before carving.

Strain the pan juices, and serve them as a sauce or toss them with the extra stuffing.

Serve with rice and roasted vegetables. The stuffing and pan juices can be tossed with the rice or scattered over the carved chicken pieces.

SAVORY SAUSAGE ROLLS

**Yield:** 13 rolls

The famous British sausage roll blends its buttery dough with a savory, meaty center (a combination that pairs *particularly* well with Forest Chutney [page 81]). A true treat at any tea-time celebration, this snack travels every bit as well as its Cornish Pasty counterpart (page 17) . . . provided, of course, that it's not gobbled up straight out of the oven!

3¾ cups all-purpose flour, plus more for the work surface

2½ cups water, divided

1 teaspoon active dry yeast

1 teaspoon kosher salt

Vegetable oil, for the baking sheet

1 pound bulk sausage meat

Forest Chutney, for serving (page 81) (optional)

Put the flour into the bowl of a stand mixer or into a large bowl, and make a well in the center. Add ½ cup of the water and the yeast to the well; then sprinkle some of the flour from the sides of the well onto the water and yeast mixture, covering it lightly. Leave until the yeast starts to bubble through this floury layer, 15 to 20 minutes.

Add the salt along the edges of the bowl, and then add the remaining 2 cups of water to the well. If mixing the dough by hand, mix with a wooden spoon or your hands until it forms a rough mass; then turn it out onto a floured work surface, and knead the dough until it is smooth and elastic, 10 to 15 minutes. If using a mixer, fit the mixer with the dough hook, and knead the dough on low speed until it is smooth and elastic, 5 to 8 minutes.

Put the dough into a clean large bowl, and cover it with plastic wrap or a damp kitchen towel. Leave it to rise in a warm spot until the dough has doubled in size, 2 to 3 hours. You can do this stage the day before baking and leave the dough to rise in the fridge overnight, removing it about 30 minutes before it is needed.

Oil a large rimmed baking sheet. Divide the dough into thirteen equal portions, each weighing about 2 ounces. Flatten each portion slightly, set a 1-ounce ball of sausage on the center, and enclose the meat completely in the dough, sealing it well and forming a log. Arrange the finished rolls, well spaced, on the prepared baking sheet, and cover them loosely with a damp kitchen towel or plastic wrap. Leave the rolls in a warm spot until they have slightly risen, 15 to 20 minutes.

Meanwhile, preheat the oven to 425°F. Bake the rolls until golden brown, about 20 minutes. They will split slightly, but the meat should stay intact. Serve them accompanied with Forest Chutney (page 81) or relishes, if desired.

PERFECTLY POTTED CHEESE

 Yield: 4 to 6 servings   **Gluten Free*, Vegetarian**

Alice is quite talented at creating extraordinary moments within a perfectly ordinary day. Naturally, she would just *adore* the aptly named potted cheese. Traditionally served with toast and comprised of a quarter pound of white cheddar cheese blended with Madeira wine, white pepper, and allspice, this spread is a staple at many proper English teas. Just don't forget to invite your favorite dormouse!

¼ pound white cheddar cheese (or similar hard, crumbly cheese)

4 tablespoons unsalted butter, at room temperature

1 teaspoon granulated sugar

½ teaspoon ground allspice

½ teaspoon white pepper

2 tablespoons Madeira wine (or sweet vermouth)

2 tablespoons clarified butter or ghee (optional)

Bread or hot toast, for serving

In the bowl of a food processor, purée the cheese until it is a smooth paste. Add the butter, sugar, allspice, white pepper, and wine; mix well. Firmly pack the mixture into a 10-ounce deep ramekin; then melt the clarified butter, and pour it on top. Cover and chill in the fridge to set.

Serve with plain or freshly toasted bread.

> **Note:** This recipe can easily be adapted to gluten-free diets if served with gluten-free bread or hot toast.

CHAPTER TWO

Down the Rabbit Hole

Alice's curiosity leads her straight into a topsy-turvy world. When our young explorer accidentally tumbles headfirst down the rabbit hole, she discovers a wonderous world in which size, direction, and even one's sense of self are all slightly skewed. But she quickly learns that she has all the tools she needs to move forward in her adventuring. After all, some things may be impassable, but nothing is *impossible*!

CURIOUSER AND CURIOUSER CHOCOLATE-COVERED DIGESTIVE COOKIES

 Yield: About 24 cookies  **Vegetarian**

There's a time and a place for responsibility. After all, chores must be done and lessons must be learned. All the same, one must also make time for a healthy dose of fun. There's no more enjoyable way to aid in the digestion of a meal than by nibbling on a delicious cookie. Digestive biscuits make a popular post-dinner treat, both in England and in Wonderland. A cookie might seem like an unlikely aid, but one must always remember: In the most fanciful of worlds, nothing would be what it is because everything would be what it isn't.

¾ cup all-purpose flour
⅓ cup whole-wheat flour
¼ cup oats
⅓ cup packed light brown sugar
¼ teaspoon baking powder
¼ teaspoon baking soda
¼ teaspoon kosher salt
½ cup salted butter
¼ cup buttermilk
6 ounces white, milk, or semisweet chocolate (optional)
Food coloring (optional)

Preheat the oven to 350°F, and prepare two baking sheets with a silicone mat or parchment. Have a variety of fluted cookie cutter shapes standing by.

In the bowl of a food processor fitted with a blade attachment, add the all-purpose flour, whole-wheat flour, and oats. Pulse several times until the oats are a coarse meal. Add the brown sugar, baking powder, baking soda, and salt. Pulse again to combine.

Cut the butter into small chunks, and add it to the flour mixture. Pulse several times, or until the butter almost disappears and you have a fine, sandy texture throughout.

Add the buttermilk, and process the mixture until the dough starts to come together.

Turn out the dough onto a lightly floured surface, and knead it into a ball. Roll out the dough to a scant ¼ inch thick, using more flour as needed to prevent sticking.

Cut out as many cookies as possible, and then reroll the scraps as needed. Place the cookies on the baking sheets, and bake for 15 to 18 minutes or until dry to the touch and golden brown. After 5 minutes, transfer the cookies to a wire rack, and allow them to cool completely.

To decorate the cookies with chocolate, gently melt the chocolate in the microwave, being careful not to overheat it. Use an offset spatula to spread a thick layer of chocolate on the top of each cookie. Smooth off any excess chocolate, and place the cookies chocolate side up on a wire rack, to set. If desired, after a minute or two, use the tines of a fork to create a wavy pattern in the chocolate.

> **Note:** A few drops of food coloring can be used to color white chocolate, if you are using it.

GROWTH POTION

 Yield: 2 servings   **Gluten Free, Vegetarian**

Even in a most unusual world, it's important to remember that if one drinks too much from a particular type of bottle, its contents are certain to disagree with one sooner or later. Luckily, this Growth Potion is *most* agreeable—and particularly delicious! With its oh-so-lovely layers and its scintillating flavor of pineapple mixed with cherries and cream soda, this glittering beverage brings a sprinkle of magic to even the most humdrum of days.

1 cup pineapple juice

One 12-ounce can cream soda

Whipped cream

4 tablespoons cherry filling from the Unbirthday Par-tea Cupcakes (page 107) (or bar cherries in syrup)

Fill two tall glasses with ice. Split the pineapple juice between the glasses. Use a spoon to layer the cream soda over the juice; you might have extra soda.

Top with whipped cream, drizzle 2 tablespoons of cherry syrup over the whipped cream, and top with a cherry.

Serve immediately.

MAGIC COOK-KEYS

Yield: About 2 dozen cookies **Vegetarian**

The road to Wonderland is burdened with obstacles—including one particularly stubborn door. Luckily, even this hurdle can be circumvented . . . provided one has the right key, of course! Wonderland wanderers will appreciate these tasty tools, which simultaneously open doorways to adventure *and* offer up an irresistibly appetizing aroma.

3 cups sifted all-purpose flour, plus more for dusting

½ teaspoon baking soda

¼ teaspoon baking powder

½ cup (1 stick) unsalted butter

½ cup dark brown sugar

3 teaspoons ground ginger

2 teaspoons ground cinnamon

½ teaspoon ground cloves

¾ teaspoon kosher salt

¾ teaspoon freshly ground black pepper

1 egg

½ cup molasses

Royal Icing (page 35)

Gray and gold food coloring (or desired colors)

Luster dust (optional)

Special Supplies:
Key-shape cookie cutter

In a large bowl, sift together the flour, baking soda, and baking powder, and set aside.

In the bowl of a stand mixer fitted with a paddle attachment, cream the butter and brown sugar on medium speed until fluffy, 1 to 2 minutes, scraping down the sides as necessary.

Add in the ginger, cinnamon, cloves, salt, and black pepper, and mix to combine.

Scrape down the sides of the bowl, and add the egg and molasses. Mix until well combined, scraping down the bowl as needed.

With the mixer on low, add in the flour mixture about 1 cup at a time, scraping the bowl as needed, until the ingredients are all incorporated.

Divide the dough in half, wrap each half in parchment, and chill for at least 1 hour.

Preheat the oven to 350°F, and prepare two baking sheets with parchment or baking mats.

On a floured surface, roll out the dough to a scant ¼ inch, and use a key-shape cookie cutter to cut out cookies.

Chill each sheet of cookies for 15 minutes, and then bake for 8 to 10 minutes until the cookies are crisp at the edges, with barely soft centers. Transfer the baking sheets to a wire rack, and allow the cookies to cool completely.

To decorate the cookies, divide the royal icing between two or more bowls, and add food coloring as desired. Flood each cookie with a base of icing, and allow it to dry completely. Pipe a key design onto each cookie. When the icing is dry, brush with luster dust, if desired.

WHITE RABBIT GRAHAM CRACKER COTTAGES

Yield: About 4 houses and about 3 cups Royal Icing **Vegetarian**

The path down the rabbit hole is filled with curiosities, from floating chairs to magical potions. Wonderland's unusual epicurean side effect—that of growing and shrinking its culinary connoisseurs—is an experience most visitors would find rather abhorrent. Although Alice has a larger-than-life experience inside the White Rabbit's home, architects of these Graham Cracker Houses will find their structures perfectly suited to their individual tastes—as it should be!

One 14-ounce box of graham crackers

Royal Icing (see below)

Brown and green food coloring (or additional colors, as desired)

Pastry bags fitted with couplers and #3 writing tips (additional tips optional)

Royal Icing:

8 cups sifted powdered sugar (about 2 pounds)

6 tablespoons meringue powder

⅔ cup water

Each House:

6 sheets of graham crackers, plus a few extra in case of breakage

About 30 mini cereal wheat squares

1 long pretzel rod

Chocolate rocks

Additional candy décor (optional)

To make the Royal Icing: In the bowl of a stand mixer fitted with a whisk attachment, combine the sifted powdered sugar and the meringue powder.

Add the water, mix on low for 1 minute, stop the mixer, and scrape down the sides. Continue to mix for another 7 to 9 minutes on low until the icing holds stiff peaks.

Split the icing into separate bowls. Leave some white, dye some a light brown to match the graham cracker, dye some a darker brown for the Tudor details, dye some green, and continue with any other colors you choose.

Continued on page 36

Continued from page 35

To build the house: Using a bread knife, cut one graham cracker sheet in half along the short perforation, creating two almost-squares, and set aside. Cut a second sheet in half the same way. Cut each square in half on the diagonal by gently sawing, to create two triangles. You need only two complete triangles for each house, so some breakage is okay.

Line a baking sheet with parchment paper. Use the light brown icing to "glue" one triangle to the slightly longer side of a graham cracker square. Place this graham cracker flat on the baking sheet, and repeat with a second square and triangle. Allow to set for about 15 minutes.

While the end pieces are flat and setting, add any details you want to them, such as a door, vines, Tudor details, and windows. You can also add details to the two whole graham cracker sheets that will make up the sides of the house.

When the icing on these pieces has set, use the light brown icing to glue the two ends to one long side. Gently hold the pieces upright for a few minutes, and then allow to set about 15 minutes. When this has set, gently attach the remaining side, and allow another 15 minutes to set.

Line each exposed edge of the house with the tan icing, and place two complete sheets along the edges of the triangle ends, making sure they "rest" on the side edges of the structure. Don't worry if a gap appears at the roof peak—the pretzel rod will cover this. Allow the graham crackers to set another 15 to 20 minutes.

When the roof is set, add the "thatch" by using dark brown frosting to "glue" the wheat squares onto the roof. Top with the pretzel beam. Use the white frosting to add the chocolate "stone work" to the base of the house. Use other frosting colors or candy to add any other desired details, such as paths, a garden, or flowers.

Allow the houses to dry completely, and then display.

"I'M REALLY IN A STEW"

 Yield: 8 servings   Gluten Free, Vegetarian, Vegan

When Alice finds herself carried away by a sea of her own sorrow, a most curious creature comes to her aid. The verily verbose (and unexpectedly helpful!) Doorknob shows the young adventurer that she isn't alone when he offers her a bite to eat. As any good voyager knows, a robust meal sets the stage for a successful expedition—and this healthy twist on a hearty classic makes for fabulous travel fare!

1 large leek

6 medium carrots (preferably multicolored)

3 medium parsnips

1 pound new potatoes

3 tablespoons olive oil

4 tablespoons rice flour

1 tablespoon paprika

1 teaspoon freshly ground black pepper

¼ teaspoon chili powder

4 cups vegetable broth

½ cup sparkling apple cider

One 15-ounce can cannellini beans

1 cup water

1 teaspoon salt

3 or 4 sprigs fresh parsley, minced, for garnish

Slice the leek in half lengthwise, and thoroughly rinse out the grit; then slice the leek crosswise. Peel the carrots and parsnips, and cut into rounds about ¼ inch thick. Scrub the potatoes, and cut into quarters.

Heat the oil in a large Dutch oven or pot over medium heat. When the oil shimmers, add the leek pieces and cook until softened, about 5 minutes. Add the potatoes, carrots, and parsnips, and stir, mixing thoroughly with the leek. Allow the vegetables to soften and the leeks to brown for 7 to 10 minutes, stirring occasionally.

In a small bowl, combine the flour, paprika, black pepper, and chili powder. Sprinkle the flour mixture over the vegetables, and stir until they are evenly coated. Cook until the flour is golden brown and fragrant, 5 to 7 minutes.

Add the broth and sparkling cider, stir the stew, and be sure to scrape up any browned bits off the bottom of the pot. Bring the stew to a boil, turn down the heat to medium-low, and simmer for about 40 minutes or until the potatoes are fork tender.

Stir in the beans, unstrained. Then fill the can approximately half full with 1 cup of water, swirl to get most of the bean liquid from the can, and pour into the stew. Stir in salt. Continue to cook until the beans are warmed through, 5 to 10 minutes.

Garnish with minced parsley, and serve immediately.

BILL THE LIZARD'S LADDER BREAD

 Yield: About 18 pretzels **Vegetarian**

One good turn deserves another. And in cooking—as in home repair!—an enthusiastic partner can make the experience all the more enjoyable. This warm and doughy delicacy is perfect to prepare with a friend who has come over for a cuppa or perhaps even helped evict an oversize houseguest. As Bill the Lizard himself might say, "At your service, Governor!"

Pretzels:

1 cup warm water, about 110°F
¼ cup dark brown sugar
1 packet (¼ ounce) rapid-rise yeast
3¼ cups all-purpose flour
1 tablespoon kosher salt
6 tablespoons cold unsalted butter, divided
1 cup sparkling apple cider vinegar
½ cup baking soda

Cinnamon Sugar:

¼ cup granulated sugar
2 teaspoons cinnamon

> **Note:** The dough must rise for 8 hours or overnight before baking.

To make the pretzels: In a medium bowl, mix together the warm water, brown sugar, and yeast. Let stand 5 to 10 minutes, until foamy.

In the bowl of a stand mixer fitted with a hook attachment, mix together the flour and salt. Cut 5 tablespoons of the butter into small pieces, and work it into the flour with a pastry cutter or your hands until it is crumbly. Add the yeast mixture, and mix on low, stopping and scraping the bowl as necessary until all the liquid has been incorporated.

Set the mixer to low (or the manufacturer's recommended setting for dough), and mix the dough until it is smooth and elastic, about 4 to 6 minutes. Remove the dough from the bowl, form it into a ball, and wrap it in plastic wrap. Refrigerate for 8 hours or overnight.

Preheat the oven to 400°F, and line two baking sheets with parchment.

On a lightly floured work surface, roll out the dough to a roughly 12-by-14-inch rectangle. Cut dough into long strips about ½ inch wide. Working with one strip at a time, cut the strip in half. Roll the first half into a long rope, and place the rope on one of the prepared sheets in a snakelike pattern, creating at least three to four hills and valleys. This creates the rungs of the ladder. Roll the second half of the strip into another long rope, and cut this one in half. Place each half on top of the rungs, creating the side rails of the ladder; press down gently to adhere. Continue to make ladders until you have used half the dough. Cover the remaining dough with a clean tea towel.

In a large, deep pot set over medium-high heat, bring 8 cups of water, the apple cider vinegar, and the baking soda to a simmer. Gently lower one or two pretzels into the water bath, and simmer for about 30 seconds. Gently hold the pretzels under the liquid, if necessary. Use a large strainer or spider to remove the pretzels, and place them onto the second baking sheet. Repeat with the remaining pretzels, and then bake in the oven for 5 minutes.

To make the cinnamon sugar: Mix the sugar and cinnamon in a small bowl. Store any leftovers in an airtight container.

While the pretzels are baking, melt the remaining 1 tablespoon butter. After baking, brush the pretzels with the butter and sprinkle them with cinnamon sugar. Rotate the tray, and bake for another 5 to 6 minutes or until the pretzels are dark golden brown.

While the first batch of pretzels is baking, form more pretzels with the remaining dough. Repeat the water bath and baking process.

WHITE RABBIT'S GARDEN CRUDITÉ

 Yield: 15 to 20 servings **Gluten Free, Vegetarian**

The White Rabbit has the lushest vegetable garden, and he is quite proud of it. His little patch of paradise is sprinkled with carrots, turnips, and delightfully fresh cucumbers. If your own garden offers up such a bounty, a vegetable crudité makes for a sensible—and salubrious!—use of excess resources. And isn't it nice when something makes sense for a change?

1 to 2 bunches thin asparagus

2 English cucumbers

2 bunches small radishes

2 bunches baby carrots, with greens intact

20 to 30 sugar snap peas

8 ounces cream cheese, softened

2 ounces crème fraîche

1 teaspoon finely minced fresh chives

½ teaspoon finely minced fresh thyme

¼ teaspoon finely minced fresh rosemary

To prepare the vegetables, start by blanching the asparagus. Snap off the tough ends of each stalk of asparagus. Fill a large pot with water, and bring to a boil over high heat. While the water is coming to a boil, fill a large bowl with cold water and ice, and have it standing by. When the water is boiling, put all the asparagus in at once, and boil for 1 minute. Remove the asparagus stalks with tongs, and immediately plunge them into the ice bath. Use the tongs to gently remove the stalks from the ice bath, and let them drain in a colander. Set aside.

Slice the cucumbers into ¼-inch slices. Slice the radishes into ¼-inch slices, leaving a few very small ones whole for garnish. Trim the carrot greens so that you have just a short bunch of stems, with few to no leaves. Gently peel.

In a medium bowl, thoroughly mix together the cream cheese and crème fraîche. Add minced chives, thyme, and rosemary, and stir until evenly distributed. Set aside.

Arrange the asparagus, cucumbers, radishes, carrots, and peas in neat garden rows on one or more serving platters; pat them dry, if necessary.

Load the cream cheese mixture into a piping bag fitted with a coupler, and have several tips standing by (such as a large petal, an open star, and a closed star). Pipe the mixture onto the vegetables, switching up the tips to add variety. If you do not have a piping bag and tips, you can spread the cream cheese mixture onto the veggies or pipe it using a sealable plastic bag with a corner snipped off.

Either serve immediately or refrigerate for up to 2 hours. Serve as an appetizer.

CHAPTER THREE

Ocean of Tears

When a larger-than-life Alice is overwhelmed by sadness, she cries a veritable ocean of tears. The heartbroken adventurer is quickly swept away in the current of her own sorrow. Fortunately, she is able to find refuge within a floating glass bottle. As Alice travels along the sea, she encounters a dancing Dodo, a jolly caucus race, and a most peculiar method of getting dry. As she discovers, the ocean is a particularly peculiar place—one she very much hopes to escape sooner rather than later!

AN OCEAN OF TEARS BLUE DRINK

 Yield: 2 servings **Gluten Free, Vegetarian**

Once Alice cried herself an ocean, she promptly declared, "Oh dear. I do wish I hadn't cried so much." This tear-inspired concoction is so delicious, one might wish it would never come to an end! Made with blue spirulina and teeming with bursts of flavor, this clever blue beverage conjures up images of drifting across the tranquil blue sea. Oh, the sailor's life!

½ cup lychee popping boba (available at specialty stores or online)

¼ teaspoon blue spirulina powder

½ teaspoon lemon zest

2 tablespoons freshly squeezed lemon juice

About 12 ounces fizzy water

Strain the boba juice into a small bowl, and set aside the pearls. Mix the spirulina powder, lemon zest, and lemon juice into the boba juice until the spirulina is incorporated. Add the pearls back in, and split the liquid between the two glasses.

Fill the glasses gently with ice, and top with fizzy water. Serve immediately with boba straws.

OF CABBAGE ROLLS AND KINGS

 Yield: 6 servings and 2½ cups mustard

The time has come to talk of cabbages and kings. But when one is adrift on the open ocean, those cabbages might just conjure up images of flotation devices, particularly if they have been molded into rolls. These savory Stuffed Cabbage Rolls (and their tangy, homemade mustard) might not work as proper life preservers, but they *will* make a splash at any dinner party—oceanside or otherwise.

Homemade Mustard:

¼ cup yellow mustard seeds
¼ cup brown mustard seeds
½ cup sparkling apple cider
1¼ cups white vinegar
1 tablespoon mixed peppercorns
2 teaspoons salt
1 teaspoon dried marjoram
⅓ cup olive oil

Stuffed Cabbage Rolls:

1 large head purple cabbage
1 tablespoon olive oil
1 large carrot, diced
1 medium yellow onion, diced
2 pounds ground beef
1 cup breadcrumbs
2 teaspoons salt
Freshly ground black pepper
1 egg
1 cup beef broth

Mustard Sauce:

1 tablespoon unsalted butter
1 shallot, finely minced
¼ cup heavy whipping cream
½ cup Homemade Mustard (see above) or good-quality stone ground mustard

> **Note:** The mustard is best made 1 week ahead of use, to allow the flavors to meld.

To make the mustard: In a nonreactive container with a tight-fitting lid, add the yellow and brown mustard seeds, apple cider, and vinegar. Seal and let sit at room temperature for 48 hours; check the contents occasionally, and cover with more cider, if necessary.

Transfer the seeds and liquid to the bowl of a food processor fitted with a blade attachment, and process for 1 minute. Add the peppercorns, salt, marjoram, and olive oil, and process for an additional 3 to 4 minutes until creamy. Some whole seeds are okay to keep in the mixture. Store in an airtight container for at least 1 week, to let the flavors meld. The mustard will keep for up to 1 month.

To make the stuffed cabbage rolls: Preheat the oven to 350°F.

Bring a large pot of water to boil. Cut the core out of the cabbage, and submerge it in the boiling water for 10 minutes. Strain, and set aside to cool.

In a small sauté pan over medium-high heat, heat the olive oil; sauté the carrot and onion for 3 to 5 minutes until the onion is translucent. Remove the contents from heat and set aside.

In a large bowl, combine the beef, breadcrumbs, salt, black pepper (to taste), cooked vegetables, and egg. Stir until well combined.

Peel off the layers of cabbage leaves, setting aside any especially torn leaves. You should have ten to twelve untorn leaves. Using a paring knife, cut off the triangular hard rib at the base of each leaf so that you can roll the leaves easily.

Scoop ¼ cup of the filling into each cabbage leaf, toward the bottom third. Fold over the sides and then the bottom, covering the meat, and then roll forward to close.

Place the cabbage rolls seam side down in a large baking dish, and add the beef broth to the bottom. Cover the cabbage rolls with the reserved cabbage leaves, and seal the pan with foil. Bake for about 1½ hours or until the internal temperature reads 160°F.

To make the mustard sauce: In a small skillet, melt the butter and sauté the shallot for 1 to 2 minutes, until translucent. Add the cream and mustard, and stir until it just comes together. Serve the sauce warm with the cabbage rolls.

THE SAILOR'S LIFE BOAT CRUDITÉ

❊ **Yield:** About 16 boats and 1½ cups hummus ❊ **Gluten Free*, Vegetarian, Vegan**

Should one ever find oneself up a proverbial creek, an errant boat would prove to be most helpful. If no such vessel can be found, then perhaps one might be made—from fresh, crisp cucumbers! These refreshing, boat-shape snacks might not provide a suitable life raft, but they make for an excellent means by which to transport dip. In the words of Wonderland's most verbose Dodo, "Ahoy! And other nautical expressions!"

Hummus:
One 15-ounce can chickpeas, drained
2 cloves garlic, minced
3 tablespoons lemon juice
¼ cup tahini paste
4 tablespoons olive oil
1½ teaspoons salt
1 teaspoon paprika

Sails:
Four 8-inch flour tortillas

To assemble the boats:
2 cucumbers
4 to 6 baby carrots

To make the hummus: Add chickpeas, garlic, lemon juice, tahini paste, oil, salt, and paprika to the bowl of a food processor. Process until the ingredients have a smooth, uniform consistency.

To make the sails: Preheat the oven to 375°F.

Cut tortillas into triangle slices, like a pizza, with approximately 1-inch bases on the outside edge. Each tortilla should yield 14 to 16 triangles.

Place slices on an ungreased baking sheet, and bake 5 to 7 minutes until crisp. Let the tortillas cool completely before using them as decoration in the cucumber boats. When they are cooled, they can be stored in an airtight container at room temperature for up to 3 days.

To assemble the boats: Peel the cucumbers, and cut them in half crosswise. Then slice each half in half again, lengthwise. Scoop out the seeds and cut each piece in half lengthwise again to create a narrow boat shape. Blot each "boat" dry. Slice the baby carrots into ¼-inch discs.

Fill each boat with approximately 2 tablespoons of hummus. Gently place the short sides of two crisp tortilla triangles close together down into the hummus, to create the "sails." Gently press a carrot disc into the hummus at the back of the boat and up on the edge for the "motor."

❊ **Wonderland Tip:** Alternatively, you can use 16 ounces of your favorite store-bought hummus.

❊ **Note:** This recipe can easily be adapted to gluten-free diets if made with gluten-free tortillas.

"WHETHER PIGS HAVE WINGS" PASTRIES

Yield: About 24 pigs in a blanket

The time has come to talk of whether pigs have wings. Flying pigs have never been seen, but that need not suggest that they don't exist. Perhaps this particular breed is simply good at hiding! Diners will delight in this clever twist on a childhood favorite, which tucks our storied pigs beneath a deliciously doughy blanket. What a fantastical meal!

1 rimmed baking sheet fitted with a baking rack

Foil

1 cup brown sugar

1 teaspoon paprika

1 teaspoon cumin

1 teaspoon freshly ground black pepper

1 pound bacon

One 17-ounce box puff pastry, defrosted according to package directions

24 mini cocktail sausages

Preheat the oven to 375°F. Cover the baking rack with foil, and place it onto the baking sheet. With a butter knife, poke holes in rows all along the foil, to allow the bacon fat to drain onto the baking sheet. Set aside.

In a large bowl, mix together the sugar, paprika, cumin, and black pepper. Add the strips of bacon, and toss to coat. Place the strips of bacon onto the foil-lined rack in a single layer, and bake for 10 minutes. Remove the bacon from the oven, and allow the strips to cool while you wrap the pigs.

Cut each sheet of puff pastry into three equal parts. Cut each one of these sections into four strips. Wrap each mini hot dog in a strip of puff pastry, and press gently to close.

Cut each strip of bacon in half, and lay it over the top of each puff pastry bundle; secure it with a toothpick through both sides. Two "wings" of bacon should rest on either side of the bundle, lying flat against the baking rack.

Return the pastries to the oven, and bake for an additional 15 minutes or until they are golden.

Allow to cool for 5 minutes. Remove the toothpicks and transfer the pastries to a serving platter, with the wings facing up.

CAUCUS RACE RAVIOLI

 **Yield:** 6 servings **Vegetarian**

Sprinting gleefully onward, Wonderland's caucus racers boldly chase what lies in front of them. Likewise, their ravioli counterparts gallantly embark on a race to be gobbled up by the most enthusiastic diner. But dinner guests need not eat *too* quickly—the winner of this race is the one who finds the single ravioli with the distinctively dyed filling! And while these flavorful morsels may be served as described, they are equally delightful when drizzled with olive oil and sprinkled with Parmesan cheese, or served with a hearty portion of pasta sauce. After all, nothing could be drier than a jolly caucus race!

Pasta Dough:

2 cups 00 flour

Pinch of kosher salt

2 large eggs plus 2 large egg yolks

1 tablespoon olive oil

1 tablespoon water

Filling:

2 cloves garlic

1 cup fresh basil leaves

15 ounces ricotta cheese

½ cup finely grated Parmesan cheese

1 tablespoon chopped sundried tomatoes

To make the pasta by hand: Place the flour on a work surface, mix in the salt, and shape the flour into a mound. Make a well in the center. Add the eggs, egg yolks, oil, and water to the well. Using a fork, beat the mixture until blended, keeping the liquid inside the well. Continue to gently beat the egg mixture, gradually drawing in the flour from the sides of the well. When the mixture is too stiff to use the fork, gently mix the dough with your fingertips, gradually drawing in more flour just until a soft, moist, but not sticky ball of dough forms. Leave behind any remaining flour by using a bench scraper to clean the work surface. Dust the work surface with flour, and knead the dough until smooth and elastic, about 10 minutes.

To make the pasta with a stand mixer: In the bowl fitted with the paddle attachment, mix 1½ cups of the flour and the salt. In a liquid measuring cup, whisk together the eggs, egg yolks, oil, and water. Slowly drizzle the egg mixture into the flour, beating on medium speed until combined, about 1 minute. Turn out the dough onto a lightly floured surface, and knead by hand until smooth and firm, adding more flour as needed, about 4 minutes.

Allow the gluten in the dough to relax before rolling the dough. Place the dough (made by any method) on a lightly floured work surface, cover it with a kitchen towel, and let it rest for 30 minutes, or wrap it in plastic and refrigerate it for up to 2 days; if the dough is refrigerated, let it stand at room temperature for 30 minutes before using.

To use a manual pasta machine, set the rollers to the widest setting. Divide the dough into three equal pieces. Using your hands or a rolling pin, flatten the dough to about ¼ inch so that it fits through the widest setting. Guide the dough through the rollers. Fold the ends of the pasta sheet over the center, like a letter, and pass it through the widest setting again, dusting it with flour as needed to prevent sticking. Fold and roll the dough again until the dough is silky smooth, three to four times.

Switch to the next-thinnest setting, and guide the dough through once. Repeat at each setting in the sequence, dusting with flour as needed, until the desired thinness is reached (6 or 7 on most pasta machines). Dust the dough with flour, and let it rest for 10 minutes before cutting. Cut the dough into 3-by-3-inch squares. Cover those squares with a towel while you make the filling.

To make the filling: In the bowl of a food processor fitted with a blade attachment, pulse the garlic and basil leaves until chopped. Reserve 1 tablespoon of the ricotta; add the rest plus the Parmesan to the basil mixture. Pulse until the mixture is well combined.

In a small bowl, mix the reserved ricotta with the sundried tomato.

To assemble, place a generous tablespoon of the filling onto half the pasta squares, dampen the edges with a bit of water, and place a second square on top. Press firmly around the filling, to remove any air. Fill the last two pasta squares with the sundried tomato filling.

Bring a large pot of salted water to a boil, and gently add ravioli three or four at a time. Cook for 2 or 3 minutes, remove the ravioli with a slotted spoon, and serve immediately. Just a drizzle of olive oil and a bit of Parmesan is all that is needed. Continue until all the ravioli are cooked.

SUN AND MOON PIZZA PIE

 **Yield:** 8 servings

In Wonderland, there exist a goodly number of contrary things: Mad Tea Parties, the Cheshire Cat, and, as we'll soon see, the frightfully rigid rules of a mild-mannered garden game. In the case of this pizza, however, contrariwise is a thing of beauty. After all, it's not every day that one peers up at the sky and sees both the sun and the moon at the very same time! Inspired by this most extraordinary of experiences, the Sun and Moon Pizza Pie represents the full cycle of a dreamer's day. Whether drifting across a moonlit world of whimsy or tiptoeing through the tulips on a golden afternoon, this vegetable-packed pizza can be enjoyed at *any* time.

1 white onion, thinly sliced
3 tablespoons olive oil, divided
1 teaspoon salt
1 Chinese eggplant, thinly sliced
1 tablespoon balsamic vinegar
½ cup shredded Parmesan cheese
1 clove garlic, peeled
1 cup basil leaves, roughly chopped
½ cup heavy whipping cream
Two 16-ounce pizza doughs
1 yellow bell pepper, cut into thin strips (save the top to cut out stars)
1 orange bell pepper, cut into thin strips
½ cup pepperoni slices (optional)
4 cups shredded mozzarella cheese

Special Tools:
Small star cookie cutter (optional)
Rimmed baking sheet

Preheat the oven to 400°F. In a bowl, toss the onions, 1½ tablespoons of the olive oil, and the salt. In a separate bowl, toss the eggplant in the remaining olive oil and the balsamic vinegar.

Still keeping them separate, place the eggplant and onions on either end of the baking sheet, and roast for 20 to 25 minutes until the eggplant is well browned and the onions are soft.

Put the Parmesan and garlic in a blender or food processor, and pulse until the mixture is well combined and the Parmesan cheese is sandy. Add the basil, and pulse multiple times until it is finely chopped. Add the cream, and pulse two or three times or until a thick paste has formed.

Raise the oven temperature to 450°F. On a lightly floured surface, roll or stretch each piece of dough to a 16-inch round, and place the dough circle on a pizza pan or large baking sheet. Split the pesto cream between both pizzas, and spread it into an even layer. Cover the pizzas in shredded mozzarella, and arrange the toppings to create the sun and moon. If desired, use the cookie cutter to cut a few stars from the reserved top of the yellow bell pepper. You can create either a sun pizza and a moon pizza or two half-and-half pizzas.

Bake the pizzas for 12 to 16 minutes, until the crust is golden brown and the cheese is bubbly.

CHAPTER FOUR

Tulgey Wood

The dark, verdant trees of Tulgey Wood appear to stretch onward without end. A peculiar set of creatures populates this forest: Each character is equal parts unconventional and unhelpful. Mome Raths offer up topsy-turvy directions, while a wayward Broomdog sweeps away the path on which Alice walks. Although its dense foliage and symphonic sea of flowers make the forest a most confounding place, one can succeed in trekking out of these tricky trees . . . as long as one receives some Very Good Advice.

TWEEDLEDEE & TWEEDLEDUM BROWNIE CAKE POPS

 Yield: About 24 cake pops   **Vegetarian**

Some of the finest combinations are also the most unexpected—logic and manners, cabbages and kings, and, in the case of *this* recipe, brownies and cake pops! Tweedledum and Tweedledee would delight in this captivating combination of *two* beloved desserts. There's nothing contrariwise about it!

Brownie Base:

12 tablespoons (1½ sticks) salted butter

4 ounces unsweetened chocolate, broken into small pieces

2 cups granulated sugar

4 eggs

1½ cups all-purpose flour

Frosting:

4 tablespoons (½ stick) salted butter

½ cup chunky peanut butter

½ cup powdered sugar

1½ teaspoons vanilla

To assemble the cake pops:

About 24 paper lollipop sticks

15 ounces yellow candy melts

10 ounces red candy melts

1½ cups (½ recipe) Royal Icing (page 35)

Blue food coloring

Pastry bags

To make the brownie base: Preheat the oven to 350°F. Line a 9-by-13-inch pan with parchment paper.

In a large microwave-safe bowl, add the butter and the chocolate. Microwave for 1 minute, stir, and then microwave for 30 seconds more, if needed. Stir until the chocolate is completely melted and smooth.

Add the sugar, and stir until combined. Add the eggs one at a time, stirring after each addition, to incorporate. Add the flour, and stir until completely incorporated.

Pour the batter into the prepared pan, and bake for 30 to 35 minutes or until a cake tester comes out mostly clean. Allow the brownies to cool for 15 minutes. Use the parchment to remove the brownies from the pan, place on a baking sheet, and refrigerate for at least 1 hour or overnight.

To make the frosting: With a mixer, beat the butter, peanut butter, and powdered sugar until the mixture is pale in color and fluffy, 1 to 2 minutes. Add the vanilla, and mix again briefly. Set aside.

Continued on page 60

Continued from page 59

 Wonderland Tip:
These can be made ahead and stored in an airtight container or slipped into individual cellophane bags and given as gifts or favors.

To assemble the cake pops: In a large bowl, break up the brownie mixture, and add 1 cup of the frosting to it. Stir to combine, making sure all of the frosting is incorporated. The mixture should start to come together like a dough. Add more frosting as needed, a tablespoon or two at a time.

Prepare a baking sheet with a baking mat or parchment. To form the pops, use a cookie scoop about 1½ inches across to scoop out a generous 2 tablespoons of the mixture. Roll the mixture between your hands to create a ball as perfectly round as possible. Place the ball on the prepared baking sheet, and insert a stick into it going almost to the bottom. Repeat until all the mixture has been used. Freeze the pops for at least 30 minutes.

When the cake pops have frozen, melt the yellow candy melts in a melting pot or microwave-safe bowl, being careful not to overheat. Dip each cake pop into the yellow, making sure it comes to the base of the stick. Shake gently to release the excess candy melt, and set the cake pop back down on the baking sheet.

When all the cake pops have been coated in yellow, melt the red candy melts. Dip each cake pop about halfway into the red candy melt, gently shake it, and set it back down on the mat.

When the candy has set completely, dye a third of the royal icing blue, and leave the rest white. Put the white icing into a pastry bag with a writing tip, or snip a small hole in the end of a bag. Pipe white collars onto the cake pops. Let set for about 30 minutes.

When the collars have completely set, put the blue icing into a pastry bag and then pipe on bow ties. Let set for about 30 minutes. When the bow ties have set, the cake pops are ready to serve.

GARDEN THISTLE ARTICHOKE DIP

 Yield: 4 to 6 servings   **Gluten Free*, Vegetarian**

Much like an artichoke, Tulgey Wood has a harsh, prickly exterior. But inside, one may find hidden pockets of warmth—and a handful of unexpectedly delightful twists. With its heady aroma, creamy texture, and savory pops of flavor, this artichoke dip embodies the spirit of Tulgey in the most delightful way. Do try *not* to get lost in it!

Two 14-ounce cans quartered artichoke hearts, drained

3 tablespoons olive oil, divided

3 tablespoons balsamic vinegar, divided

1 large shallot

1 bunch flat leaf parsley, divided

8 tablespoons unsalted butter, softened, divided

One 8-ounce block cream cheese, softened

Juice of 1 lemon

1 teaspoon salt

Freshly ground black pepper

1 baguette, sliced on an angle

Four to six 10-ounce ramekins, or one 9-inch baking or pie dish

Preheat the oven to 400°F.

On a rimmed baking sheet, toss the artichokes with 1 tablespoon olive oil and 1 tablespoon balsamic vinegar. Roast the artichokes for 15 to 20 minutes until they start to brown. Remove from the oven, and allow to cool completely.

While the artichokes are cooling, put the shallot and six stems of parsley in the bowl of a food processor. Pulse until finely chopped.

Add 6 tablespoons of the butter and the cream cheese, lemon juice, salt, and black pepper (to taste) to the food processor, and process until well combined. Add the cooled artichoke hearts; pulse until the mixture is well combined and the artichoke is chopped. Grease the baking dish or ramekins with the remaining butter, and fill two-thirds of the way with the dip mixture, smoothing the top.

Preheat the oven to 350°F. In a large bowl, toss the baguette slices with the remaining 2 tablespoons olive oil and balsamic vinegar. Arrange the baguette slices on a baking sheet, and place both the baking sheet and the dip in the oven. Remove the baguette after 5 to 7 minutes or when crisp, and set aside. Bake the dip for 25 to 30 minutes or until puffed and starting to brown.

Arrange some of the baguette slices like petals: Press them into the center of the dip, place them on a cutting board, and arrange additional parsley stems and baguette slices.

> **Note:** This recipe can easily be adapted to gluten-free diets if served with a gluten-free baguette.

CHESHIRE CAT PANNA COTTA

 Yield: 4 servings   **Gluten Free**

When making this playful twist on a classic panna cotta, it doesn't really matter which way you go. Any seasonal fruit will do, although strawberry and blackberry are always forest favorites. Whatever you choose, be sure to set aside a bowl of cream to appease your favorite feline. Looking for him? Why, he went *that* way . . .

Blackberry Panna Cotta:
1 envelope gelatin
1 cup milk, divided
2 cups blackberries, rinsed
½ cup superfine sugar
2-inch piece of ginger, peeled and thickly sliced
1 cup heavy whipping cream

Strawberry Panna Cotta:
2 cups strawberries, rinsed and hulled
½ cup superfine sugar
2 sprigs of basil
1 envelope gelatin
1 cup milk, divided
1 cup heavy whipping cream

Garnish:
Pastry bag and parchment paper
1 cup white chocolate chips
About 8 blackberries
2 strawberries

Special Tools:
Four 10-ounce dessert cups or glasses

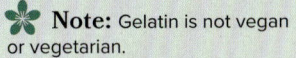 **Note:** Gelatin is not vegan or vegetarian.

To make the Blackberry Panna Cotta: In a small bowl, allow the gelatin to bloom over ½ cup of the milk.

In the bowl of a food processor fitted with a blade attachment, add the blackberries and pulse until puréed. Add the purée to a medium saucepan over medium heat. Add the sugar and ginger pieces, and stir to combine.

Cook the mixture over medium heat, stirring until the sugar is completely dissolved. Add the cream and the remaining ½ cup of milk.

Continue to stir, and cook until the mixture is almost scalding, 3 to 5 minutes; then remove from heat. Strain the mixture through a fine mesh strainer, and return it to the pot, discarding the solids.

Whisk the gelatin with its milk, and add this to the pot. Return the pot to medium-low heat, and continue to whisk until the mixture is dissolved.

Strain the mixture again into a heatproof measuring cup.

Pour a layer of the Blackberry Panna Cotta into the bottom of each dessert cup, about ½ inch deep. Refrigerate the dessert cups, and leave the extra Blackberry Panna Cotta in a cool place.

To make the Strawberry Panna Cotta:
Begin by pulsing the strawberries in the food processor until they are puréed. Add the strawberry purée to a clean medium pot with the superfine sugar and basil sprigs, and repeat steps 1 and 3 through 5.

When the first layer of Blackberry Panna Cotta has chilled at least 30 minutes, gently pour a layer of strawberry about ½ inch deep, being careful to pour it near the edges. Chill another 30 minutes, and then repeat with the remaining blackberry layer. Chill again, and finish with the final strawberry layer, to fill the dessert cups.

Continued on page 64

Continued from page 63

> ✳ **Note:** This panna cotta can be made up to 3 days ahead. Serve chilled, and set the garnishes on top right before serving.

To make the garnish: To make the Cheshire Cat's smile and eyes, draw four circles on a large piece of parchment paper the size of the mouth of the dessert cups. Place the parchment on a baking sheet.

Put the chocolate chips in a pastry bag, twist the end to close, and microwave 30 seconds at a time. Between each burst, massage the chocolate chips, to help them melt. When the chips are completely melted, use the circles as a guide to pipe the smile of the cat; fill in the smile with chocolate. Repeat to create four smiles. Tap the cookie sheet several times, to settle the chocolate. Using a butter knife, drag deep vertical lines up and down the smile, from one end to the other, to create large teeth; then drag the knife from corner to corner, to create two rows. Be sure to not break the top and bottom edges. Pipe eight circles about the size of a quarter, to create the eyes. Cut the ends off the blackberries, and set them in the bottoms or centers of the eyes. Allow to set for 15 minutes. Carefully peel off the parchment, and store the dessert cups in an airtight container until serving. When ready to serve, slice two strawberries and place two slices per cup as ears, and place on the chocolate eyes and smile.

GOLDEN AFTERNOON GREENS

 Yield: 4 to 6 servings **Gluten Free, Vegetarian, Vegan**

A romp through the forest offers the ideal opportunity to appreciate nature's gifts. And what better way to honor Tulgey Wood than by preparing a dish overflowing with fragrant flora? A generous portion of mixed baby lettuce leaves offers a lush base for a dazzling array of edible flora and a deliciously savory dressing. (Get-up-in-the-morning glories are optional!) Crisp, light, and with just a hint of sweetness, this salad is sure to make any daffodil dizzy with delight.

Dressing:
- ½ teaspoon saffron threads
- 3 tablespoons olive oil
- 3 tablespoons champagne vinegar
- 1 teaspoon minced shallot
- ¼ teaspoon kosher salt

Salad:
- About 8 ounces mixed baby lettuces
- ¼ cup shelled pistachios
- About 1 cup assorted edible flowers (such as nasturtium, johnny jump ups, dianthus, snapdragon, and society garlic) or flowering herbs (such as lavender, thyme, or coriander)

To make the dressing: Toast the saffron threads on a dry pan by heating a small skillet on the stove until it gets very hot. Remove the pan from heat, add the saffron threads, and stir them gently until fragrant, about 2 minutes.

Put the oil into a medium bowl. Whisk in the saffron, vinegar, shallot, and salt.

To make the salad: In a large salad bowl, combine the lettuces, pistachios, and flowers and herbs, and toss with the dressing to coat. Serve immediately.

FANCIFUL FRUIT SHRUBS

 Yield: About 2 cups strained, or 4 cups with fruit   **Gluten Free, Vegetarian, Vegan**

If you find your fruit trees to be *especially* bountiful, a batch of shrubs provides a marvelous means of preserving a harvest. Simply combine a batch of berries, peaches, or plums with a handful of not-so-secret ingredients, and wait for this recipe to work its magic. In no time at all, you'll be sipping on a scintillating beverage—umbrella birds optional!

Raspberry-Rose Shrub:
1 cup frozen raspberries (or fresh, if in season)
1 cup granulated sugar
1 cup champagne vinegar
¼ teaspoon rose water

Peach-Vanilla Shrub:
2 cups frozen peach slices (or fresh, if in season)
1 cup granulated sugar
1 cup apple cider vinegar
1 vanilla bean

> **Note:** Fruit shrubs can be enjoyed unstrained, and the fruit chunks are delicious. Berry shrubs are better strained because of the abundance of seeds. Enjoy shrubs by using them to flavor iced teas, fizzy water, champagne, or dressings or sauces.

To make the Raspberry-Rose Shrub: In a medium bowl, combine the raspberries, sugar, vinegar, and rose water. Stir until the sugar is completely dissolved.

Pour the mixture into a container with an airtight seal, and refrigerate for at least 48 hours and up to 1 week, to allow the vinegar to mellow and the fruit to infuse.

If desired, strain the mixture through a fine mesh strainer, return it to a container with an airtight lid, and store it in the refrigerator for up to 2 months.

To make the Peach-Vanilla Shrub: Combine the peach, sugar, and apple cider vinegar in a blender, and pulse until the peach is finely chopped.

Split the vanilla bean, and then add the vanilla bean, seeds, and pod to the mixture. Transfer the mixture to an airtight container, and refrigerate for least 48 hours and up to 1 week, to allow the vinegar to mellow and the fruit to infuse.

If desired, strain the mixture through a fine mesh strainer, return it to a container with an airtight lid, and store it in the refrigerator for up to 2 months.

Get creative and try different variations—strawberry-lavender, blackberry-ginger, plum-peppercorn, or many other combinations. Shrubs are a great way to preserve farmers' market fruit. Different vinegar combinations can also create additional flavor profiles.

"I'M LATE!" QUICK ROAST VEGETABLES

 Yield: 6 servings as an entrée, up to 8 servings as a side   **Gluten Free, Vegetarian, Vegan***

Tulgey Wood is rich in produce, from the root vegetables that grow among the trees, to the carrots popping up in the White Rabbit's garden. But when a simple salad just won't do, this unexpected option provides a healthful, savory side. Warm Indian spices are offset by a cool, minted yogurt, proving that, even in a curious world, the right combinations are anything but nonsense.

Yogurt Dip:

1 cup Greek yogurt or nondairy substitute

1 cup loosely packed mint leaves, finely minced

½ teaspoon salt

2 teaspoons fresh lemon juice

1 tablespoon rice wine vinegar

Vegetables:

About 3 pounds of vegetables, such as carrots, parsnips, cauliflower, Brussels sprouts, and yellow onion

½ cup ghee, melted

2 teaspoons Madras curry powder

1 teaspoon garlic powder

1 teaspoon paprika

½ teaspoon ground cumin

½ teaspoon ground coriander

2 teaspoons kosher salt

Preheat the oven to 450°F, and have two rimmed baking sheets standing by.

To make the yogurt dip: In a small bowl, mix together the Greek yogurt, mint leaves, salt, lemon juice, and rice wine vinegar. Cover and refrigerate until serving. This can be done up to a day ahead.

To make the vegetables: Scrub clean any root vegetables, such as carrots or parsnips, but do not peel. Trim the ends, and cut the vegetables into chunks about 2 inches in length. Break down the cauliflower into florets, discarding the leaves and the core. Remove any damaged guard leaves from the Brussels sprouts, trim the ends, and cut them in half. Onions can be peeled and quartered.

In a large bowl, mix the melted ghee with the curry powder, garlic powder, paprika, cumin, coriander, and salt. Toss the flavored ghee with the vegetables, to coat evenly, and turn out the seasoned vegetables onto the baking pans in single layers. Turn the Brussels sprout halves cut side down, for extra delicious browning. Roast for 20 to 25 minutes or until fork tender.

As a main, serve over rice with the minted yogurt, or serve as is for a delicious side. This recipe pairs well with Her Royal Majesty's Crown Roast (page 116) and Forest Chutney (page 81), or Perfect Pistachio Stuffed Chicken (page 22).

 **Note:** For a vegan option, use your favorite dairy-free yogurt and swap the ghee for coconut oil or avocado oil.

WHITE RABBIT'S QUICK CHANGE OATS

 Yield: 6 servings   **Gluten Free*, Vegetarian, Vegan***

Everyone knows that breakfast is the most important meal of the day—that's true for caterpillars, white rabbits, and people alike. This foresty twist on a tried-and-true staple is the perfect dish to serve to any breakfast companion. With hints of nutmeg and a generous heaping of carrots, this oatmeal offers a quick, energy-packed meal that tastes just like carrot cake. Oh, my fur and feathers!

Toppings:
½ cup walnuts
½ cup crème fraîche or sour cream
2 tablespoons brown sugar

Oatmeal:
1 teaspoon cinnamon
½ teaspoon nutmeg
½ teaspoon ginger
¼ teaspoon allspice
2 cups old-fashioned oats
3½ cups oat milk
¼ teaspoon salt
½ cup golden raisins
1 cup shredded carrot

> **Note:** This recipe can easily be adapted to gluten-free diets if made with gluten-free oats and vegan diets if served without creme fraiche or sour cream.

To make the toppings: Heat a medium dry skillet over medium-high heat, add the walnuts, and stir for 1 minute. Remove the pan from heat, and continue to stir until the walnuts are just beginning to brown and are fragrant, 1 to 2 minutes. Transfer to a small serving bowl.

In a separate small serving bowl, combine the crème fraîche or sour cream with the brown sugar, and whisk to combine. Cover the mixture, and refrigerate until serving.

To make the oatmeal: Add the cinnamon, nutmeg, ginger, and allspice to a large saucepan on medium-high heat. Stir to combine, coating the bottom of the pan. Add the oats, and stir thoroughly to combine. Continue stirring until the oats and spices are toasted and fragrant, 2 to 3 minutes.

Add the oat milk and salt, and stir to combine. Bring to a boil, stirring occasionally. When the mixture is at a boil, turn it down to a simmer, add the raisins, and cook for 3 minutes. Add the shredded carrot, and cook for an additional 2 minutes or to the desired tenderness.

To serve, ladle the oatmeal into bowls, alongside the walnuts and cream topping.

POCKET WATCH CUPCAKES

 Yield: About 36 cupcakes   **Vegetarian**

No time to say hello or goodbye? A tasty timepiece might just be in order! These carrot cake confections look like a conventional clock, but their refreshingly sweet frosting offers an instant escape from even the most banal responsibilities. Pocket Watch Cupcakes ensure that one never loses track of time . . . that is, until dessert is served!

Cupcakes:

2⅔ cups all-purpose flour
2 cups sugar
1 tablespoon baking soda
2 teaspoons baking powder
2 teaspoons cinnamon
2 teaspoons ground ginger
1 teaspoon clove
1 teaspoon salt
5 large eggs
1⅓ cups vegetable oil
3 cups freshly grated carrot
1½ cups golden raisins

Frosting and Assembly:

18 ounces white chocolate
Three 8-ounce packages cream cheese, softened
1½ cups unsalted butter, softened
2 tablespoons fresh lemon juice
1 tablespoon vanilla extract
¼ teaspoon salt
About 1 cup gold sanding sugar
Black food coloring
2 black licorice vines, about 9 inches long
Candy pearls (optional)

Special Tools:

Pastry bag and #3 writing tip

To make the cupcakes: Preheat the oven to 350°F, and line two standard muffin pans with gold foil liners.

In the bowl of a stand mixer fitted with a paddle attachment, stir together the flour, sugar, baking soda, baking powder, cinnamon, ginger, clove, and salt.

In a medium bowl, whisk the eggs; then add them to the dry ingredients, along with the oil. Stir on low until the ingredients are well combined, scraping the bowl as needed. Stir in the carrot and raisins.

Fill each liner two-thirds full, and bake for 20 to 25 minutes, rotating halfway through, until a cake tester comes out clean. Allow the cupcakes to cool completely before frosting.

To make the frosting: In a double boiler or a microwave-safe bowl, gently melt the chocolate and set aside. If using a microwave, melt in 30-second bursts, stirring in between each one.

In the bowl of a stand mixer, cream together the cream cheese and butter until light and fluffy, 1 to 2 minutes.

Add the melted chocolate in three to four batches, mixing on medium speed between each addition and scraping down the sides of the bowl. When all the chocolate has been incorporated, add the lemon juice, vanilla, and salt. Mix on medium-high for about 1 minute.

Put the sanding sugar in a wide, shallow dish. Reserve about 1 cup of frosting. Using an offset spatula, frost each cupcake with a flat, smooth surface.

Dip two cupcakes into the sanding sugar, covering their tops completely. Leave seventeen cupcakes plain, and dip the remaining cupcakes in sugar just around the edges. These will create the outside of the watch.

Dye the reserved frosting black, and pipe the numbers 1 through 12 on twelve cupcakes, one number each.ww Pipe the word *I'm* onto one cupcake, and pipe the letters for *late* on four separate cupcakes.

Arrange all the cupcakes on a large cake board, creating the center of the pocket watch with one gold cupcake surrounded by the "I'm Late" cupcakes, and then using the numbered cupcakes to create the face of the watch. Use the remaining gold-rimmed cupcakes to create the frame of the watch, and use the remaining all-gold cupcake for the fob at the top. Place the licorice watch hands in place, trimming one to be the short hand, and pipe arrows at the ends. Decorate with pearls, if using them.

CATERPILLAR CROSTINI

 Yield: About 40 crostini   **Gluten Free*, Vegetarian**

Wonderland's mushrooms are the most extraordinary fungi. They make a human shrink (or grow!), while also providing a comfortable perch for Tulgey Wood's ever-curious caterpillar. This Smoked Mushroom Crostini would make for a rather stiff sitting spot, but its complimentary flavors are guaranteed to delight even the most critical epicurean. With hints of garlic and nutmeg, and a spot of Chèvre cheese, this savory sautéed treat is a positively wonderous snack for caterpillars and humans alike!

3 tablespoons unsalted butter

4 cloves garlic, minced

8 ounces mushroom varieties, such as oyster, cremini, shiitake, enoki, or clamshell

½ teaspoon salt

About ¼ teaspoon freshly grated nutmeg

3 bay leaves

4 ounces Chèvre cheese

1 sourdough baguette, sliced

About 2 tablespoons olive oil, for brushing the baguette

Preheat the oven to 400°F. Have a rimmed baking sheet standing by.

In a deep sauté pan with a tight-fitting lid, melt the butter. When the butter foams, add the garlic; sauté until fragrant, 1 to 2 minutes. Add the mushrooms, and sauté until they begin to brown, 5 to 7 minutes. Add the salt and nutmeg, and sauté a few minutes more until soft. Remove from heat.

Build a foil tray for the bay leaves. Push the mushrooms to the side of the pan, creating a spot for the tray. Place the tray in the bottom of the pan. Use a long match to light the bay leaves, and immediately cover with the lid, leaving a slight gap on the opposite side of the bay leaves. When the fire goes out, close the lid completely. Allow to smoke for 5 minutes.

Brush the baguette slices with the olive oil, and toast for 5 minutes or until crisp at the edges.

Remove from the oven. When cool to handle, spread with a thin layer of Chèvre and top with about 1 teaspoon of mushrooms. Bake again for 4 to 5 minutes. Serve immediately.

> **Note:** This recipe can easily be adapted to gluten-free diets if made with a gluten-free baguette.

MOROCCAN CHICKEN AND OLIVES

 Yield: 6 to 8 servings   **Gluten Free***

The Caterpillar is one of the most curious residents of Tulgey Wood. His Socratic method of speech often leaves his companions confused, but even this circuitous conversationalist would approve of Moroccan Chicken and Olives. This traditional Middle Eastern dish offers a tangy blend of paprika, cumin, and coriander seeds. It's perfect for diners of all sizes—from 3 inches tall upward!

2 teaspoons paprika

2 teaspoons ground cumin

½ teaspoon ground ginger

½ teaspoon whole coriander seeds

½ teaspoon turmeric

½ teaspoon ground nutmeg

Freshly ground black pepper

Zest of 1 lemon

8 skin-on, bone-in chicken thighs

2 tablespoons olive oil

1 cup vegetable stock

1 bunch parsley, divided

2 yellow onions, cut into large chunks

One 10-ounce jar garlic-stuffed olives, drained

Cooked rice or couscous, for serving (optional)

Preheat the oven to 375°F.

In a small bowl, mix together the paprika, cumin, ginger, coriander seeds, turmeric, nutmeg, black pepper (to taste), and lemon zest. Rub the mixture under and into the skin of each chicken thigh.

In a large Dutch oven set over medium-high heat, heat the olive oil until shimmery. Add the chicken thighs (in batches, if necessary), and brown with the skin side down, about 5 minutes, or until the thighs are a deep golden brown. Remove to a plate and repeat until all the chicken thighs have been browned.

Add the vegetable stock to the pan, and use it to deglaze the bottom; then bring to a simmer.

Reserve about ½ cup of the parsley leaves for serving; place the rest of the bunch, stems included, into the bottom of the pan. Cover with the onions and chicken thighs, and then scatter the olives over the top.

Put the lid on the Dutch oven, and bake in the oven for 30 minutes. After 30 minutes, remove the lid and bake another 10 to 15 minutes or until the internal temperature reaches 165°F.

Roughly chop the reserved parsley leaves, sprinkle over the chicken, and serve on a bed of rice or couscous.

> **Note:** This recipe can easily be adapted to gluten-free diets if served with rice instead of couscous.

A-E-I-O SOUP

 Yield: 6 servings   **Gluten Free*, Vegetarian, Vegan***

Whoever said one mustn't play with one's food was *clearly* misinformed. After all, there's no finer way to spend the day than by being creative—and mealtimes should be no exception. This Alphabet Soup offers the ideal opportunity to ask a dining mate, "Who are you?" . . . using an excessive quantity of vowels, of course.

2 cups vegetable broth

1 ounce dried porcini mushrooms

2 tablespoons olive oil

2 tablespoons salted butter

1 yellow onion, minced

2 cloves garlic, minced

2 teaspoons salt

1 teaspoon dry thyme

Freshly ground black pepper

3 cups water

1 cup (about 7 ounces) alphabet pasta

> **Note:** This recipe can easily be adapted to gluten-free diets if made with gluten-free pasta and vegan if made with a vegan butter instead of real butter.

In a small saucepan or microwave-safe measuring cup, heat the vegetable broth until very hot, about 2 minutes. Remove from heat, add the dried porcini mushrooms, and let soak for at least 10 minutes.

In a small stock pot over medium-high heat, add the olive oil and butter. When the butter begins to foam, add the minced onions and garlic. Sauté, stirring frequently, until the onions are very soft and beginning to caramelize, 10 to 15 minutes.

Place a strainer over the stock pot, and pour in the broth. Squeeze the mushrooms as dry as possible by pressing them against the strainer; then mince the mushrooms and add them to the pot along with the salt, thyme, and black pepper (to taste). Simmer over medium heat for 10 to 15 minutes, to allow the flavors to meld.

Add the water to the pot, and bring the soup to a boil. Add the pasta, and boil for 9 to 11 minutes or until the pasta is the desired tenderness. Serve immediately.

MUSHROOM PERCH PIE

 Yield: 6 mini pies **Vegetarian**

When foraging through the forest, one might stumble upon a flurry of mushrooms. And while some mushrooms have most peculiar properties (and have been known to induce sudden changes in stature), most fungi are fairly benign—and best served in a pie. This nature-inspired dish blends hints of onions, cloves, and parsley into one delightful, flaky pastry-coated crust. But *do* be careful not to eat those pesky mushrooms from the wrong side—unless a growth spurt is in order!

Pie Crust:

2½ cups all-purpose flour

1 teaspoon kosher salt

½ cup unsalted butter, very cold

¼ cup solid vegetable shortening, very cold

⅓ cup ice water

Filling:

1 tablespoon salted butter

1 tablespoon olive oil

½ yellow onion, diced

12 ounces mushrooms, sliced

½ teaspoon freshly ground black pepper

½ teaspoon salt

2 large garlic cloves, minced

1 tablespoon finely minced parsley

1 ounce Gruyère cheese, finely grated

Six 4-inch tart pans

Horseradish cream, for serving (optional)

To make the pie crust: Line a baking sheet with parchment paper. In a large bowl, combine the flour and kosher salt. Cut the cold butter and the shortening into small pieces. Using a pastry cutter or two forks, work the butter and shortening into the flour mixture until all the pieces are pea size or smaller.

Add the ice water a little bit at a time, and use the pastry cutter to bring the dough together. As the dough starts to come together, switch to your hands or a spatula, using up to ½ cup of water, until the dough just comes together.

Split the dough in half, turn out the dough onto a floured surface, and roll it out to about ⅛ inch thick. Cut out six circles 5½ inches in diameter. Gently press each circle into the bottom of the tart pans, shaping the dough into the fluted sides.

Roll out the second half of the dough, and cut six 4-inch circles. Transfer these circles and the tart pans to the baking sheet, and refrigerate while you prepare the filling.

To make the filling: In a large sauté pan over medium-high heat, melt the butter with the oil until the butter foams. Add the onion, and cook until softened, 3 to 5 minutes. Add the mushrooms to the pan, and stir to thoroughly mix them with the cooked onions. Lower the heat to medium-low. Sauté the mushrooms until most of the liquid has evaporated out of them, stirring occasionally, 10 to 15 minutes.

Return the heat to medium, and add the black pepper, salt, and garlic. Stir and sauté until the garlic is fragrant, about 1 minute. Remove pan from heat, and stir in the parsley and Gruyère cheese.

Preheat the oven to 425°F while allowing the mixture to cool for about 5 minutes.

Remove the tart shells and tops from the refrigerator. Spoon a generous 3 tablespoons of filling into each crust, place the top crust on, and use the overhang to pleat the crust closed. Arrange the tart pans on the baking sheet, and cut two vent slits into the top of each crust. Bake for 20 to 25 minutes or until golden brown.

Remove the baking sheet from the oven, and allow the tart pans to cool on the baking sheet. Serve the tarts warm or at room temperature, with optional horseradish cream.

Tarts can be stored for 3 days in an airtight container.

TULGEY WOOD FOREST CAKE

 Yield: 10 to 12 servings    Vegetarian

Tulgey Wood is a peculiar place. It stands mostly in darkness, with a tree line so dense that nary a sunbeam can peek through. But despite its perpetual twilight, the forest is peppered with unexpected bright spots, from the Mad Hatter's tea table to the White Rabbit's cottage. And just like the woods of Wonderland, this rich Forest Cake offers bursts of spicy cloves within its spongy, cinnamon-rich layers. Molded into a log and topped with touches of hand-carved bark, pistachio and pepita moss, and marzipan mushrooms, this imaginative cake brings a touch of the woods straight to any table. How very curious, indeed!

Cake:

¾ cup sifted all-purpose flour
1 teaspoon baking powder
2 teaspoons ground ginger
2 teaspoons cinnamon
½ teaspoon clove
¼ teaspoon salt
¼ cup heavy whipping cream
¼ cup dark brown sugar
⅓ cup molasses
2 tablespoons unsalted butter
4 large eggs
½ cup granulated sugar

Molasses Soaking Syrup:

2 tablespoons molasses
¼ cup hot water
¼ teaspoon freshly ground black pepper

Cream Cheese Filling:

8 ounces block cream cheese, softened
4 tablespoons unsalted butter
½ cup brown sugar
2 teaspoons vanilla

To make the cake: Grease a jelly roll pan, and cover it in parchment paper. Preheat the oven to 400°F.

In a medium bowl, sift together the flour, baking powder, ginger, cinnamon, clove, and salt. Set aside.

In a small saucepan, heat the cream, brown sugar, molasses, and butter. Stir until the butter is melted, the sugar is dissolved, and the molasses is incorporated. Remove the saucepan from heat, and have it standing by.

In the bowl of a stand mixer fitted with a whisk attachment, combine the eggs and granulated sugar. Whip on high until the mixture is light in color and the consistency of soft whipped cream.

Add the flour mixture, and fold in until well combined. Repeat by adding the cream mixture and folding again until well combined.

Pour the batter into the jelly roll pan, and spread it into an even layer. Bake for 8 to 10 minutes or until a cake tester comes out clean and the sponge bounces back when pressed. Be careful not to overbake. Allow the cake to cool completely on a wire rack, and then cover it with a barely damp cloth while you make the other components.

To make the molasses soaking syrup: In a small bowl, stir together the molasses, water, and black pepper, to combine. Set aside.

Continued on page 80

Continued from page 79

Frosting:

8 ounces semisweet chocolate, broken into chunks

1½ cups heavy whipping cream, divided

2 tablespoons honey

½ cup powdered sugar

Cake Decorations:

Crushed pistachios and pepitas as moss

Marzipan mushrooms

Modeling chocolate leaves, bugs, and flowers

To make the cream cheese filling: In the bowl of a stand mixer fitted with a paddle attachment, combine the cream cheese, butter, sugar, and vanilla. Beat until smooth and fluffy. Set aside.

To assemble the cake: Have a serving platter or cutting board standing by. Turn out the cake onto a silicone baking mat or a large piece of parchment paper. Use a pastry brush to brush the entire surface of the cake with the molasses soaking syrup. Note that you might not need all the syrup.

Spread the cream cheese filling in an even layer edge to edge over the top of the cake. Starting at a long side and using the baking mat as a brace, gently begin to roll the cake into a log. Take care to start with a tight spiral. When the cake is rolled, place it seam side down on the serving platter or cutting board. Refrigerate the cake while you make the frosting, or at least 30 minutes.

To make the frosting: Place the chocolate chunks in a microwave-safe bowl, and pour ½ cup of the cream over them. Microwave for 1 minute, and then let stand for 3 to 4 minutes more. Stir until all the chocolate is melted into the cream. Stir in the honey, and set aside.

In the bowl of a stand mixer fitted with a whisk attachment, whip the remaining cup of cream and the powdered sugar until soft peaks form. Add the chocolate cream mixture, and continue to beat until soft peaks form again.

Use an offset spatula to frost the cake from end to end without covering the spirals. Create a bark texture as you go by leaving swirls and indents in the frosting. When the cake is frosted, cut 1- to 2-inch slices off each end, and use more frosting to adhere these to the log, as desired. If you like, cut a second slice from one end, at an angle, to create a mini standing log.

Decorate with the crushed pistachios and pepitas as moss; place the mushrooms, leaves, flowers, and bugs as desired.

Chill until serving. Let the cake stand at room temperature for 30 minutes before serving.

Forest Chutney

❁ **Yield:** About 4 cups   ❁ **Gluten Free, Vegetarian, Vegan**

When listing the most quintessentially British foods, it's important to include chutney. This fruit-and-spice laden condiment is one of the best-known English delicacies and is certainly something Alice would serve to her friends. Cinnamon, mustard seeds, and dried apricot combine here to create an explosion of earthy flavors, while simultaneously showcasing the many fine bounties of Tulgey Wood.

Zest and juice of 3 large oranges

1 cup apple cider vinegar

2½ cups dark brown sugar

1 tablespoon yellow mustard seeds

1 tablespoon coriander seeds

2 cinnamon sticks, broken into pieces

½ teaspoon red pepper flakes

1 teaspoon salt

½ teaspoon freshly ground black pepper

2 pounds firm pears (such as Bosc or Anjou), peeled, cored, and sliced

1 yellow onion, diced

4 cloves black garlic

3-inch piece of ginger, peeled and diced

1 cup (about 6 ounces) dried apricots, chopped

1 cup golden raisins

1 cup apple juice

In a large nonreactive pot over medium heat, combine the zest and juice of the oranges with the vinegar, brown sugar, mustard seeds, coriander seeds, cinnamon sticks, red pepper flakes, salt, and black pepper. Stir until the sugar is dissolved.

When the sugar is dissolved, add in the pears and the onion. Stir to combine, and bring to a simmer.

Peel the black garlic, and smash it with the flat side of a knife until it is a smooth, jammy consistency. Scrape it into the pot, and stir. Add the ginger, apricot, and raisins.

Continue to simmer for 45 minutes to an hour, stirring frequently to resubmerge the pears. Add the apple juice, and simmer for another 30 to 45 minutes. The chutney is ready when the pears are translucent and tender, and the liquid has thickened enough to coat the back of the spoon.

Ladle the chutney into clean jars or a heatproof, airtight container, and refrigerate. The chutney will last up to 1 month in the refrigerator. It pairs well with Perfectly Potted Cheese (page 25), Curiously Cornish Pasties (page 17), and Her Royal Majesty's Crown Roast (page 116).

CROCODILE GOLDEN SCALE BEETS

 Yield: About 6 servings   **Gluten Free, Vegetarian**

How doth the little crocodile improve a tasty meal?
By pairing wondrous flavors that will make his diners squeal.
How cheerfully they all shall grin, when dining on such treats—
As tangy, tasty salads made of bright golden scale beets.

10 to 12 ounces small golden beets
¼ cup golden balsamic vinegar
2 tablespoons orange juice, divided
½ tablespoon orange zest
1 tablespoon minced shallot
¼ teaspoon granulated sugar
¼ teaspoon kosher salt, plus a bit more for the greens
⅛ teaspoon ground coriander
½ tablespoon olive oil
Freshly ground black pepper
6 to 8 ounces microgreens
4 ounces Chèvre cheese

> **Note:** Save your fresh beet tops, and sauté them with olive oil, butter, and garlic, much as you would chard.

Preheat the oven to 400°F.

Trim off the tops of the beets (reserve the tops), and gently trim off the root, leaving as much of the point as possible. Scrub the beets clean, and place them in an ovenproof pan with ½ inch water; cover tightly with foil. Cook until the beets are fork tender, 20 to 25 minutes.

Remove the beets from the cooking water, and allow them to completely cool. When they have cooled, place the beets onto their flat trimmed tops, and slice into ¼-inch pieces lengthwise. Place the pieces in a large shallow bowl.

Whisk together vinegar, 1 tablespoon of the orange juice, orange zest, shallot, sugar, salt, and coriander. Pour the liquid over the beet pieces, and let the beets marinate for at least 15 minutes.

In a separate large bowl, whisk together the oil, the remaining tablespoon of orange juice, and the salt and black pepper (to taste). Toss with greens.

Crumble the Chèvre across a large, shallow, serving platter. Scatter greens over the Chèvre to create a bed for the beet "crocodile."

Place the beet pieces in an overlapping pattern to create the scales of the crocodile; save the more pointed pieces for the top of the tail and teeth.

BREAD AND BUTTERFLY TOAST

 Yield: 4 to 6 servings  **Vegetarian**

Magic is *everywhere*: One must simply just know how to cook it up. With a little imagination—and some creatively crafted bread—any breakfast can be a true morning glory. An ordinary dining table becomes an enchanted forest when loaded with plates of Bread and Butterfly Toast. After all, many things can be learned from the flowers—from sunrise straight through to the golden afternoon!

6 brioche rolls or 1 brioche loaf
1 cup milk
½ cup half and half
6 eggs
4 tablespoons salted butter, melted, plus more for the pan
1 tablespoon vanilla bean paste
1 to 2 tablespoons "I'm in a Jam" Homemade Strawberry-Lemon Jam (page 105) (optional)
1 pound strawberries, hulled and sliced
½ cup Mock Clotted Cream (page 103) (optional)

Have two baking sheets standing by. Preheat the oven to **225°F**.

Slice each brioche roll into ¼-inch slices, and place them in a single layer on the baking sheets. Gently toast the brioche slices until they just start to crisp (but not brown), about 5 minutes.

While the brioche is toasting, prepare the egg custard. In a wide low dish, thoroughly whisk together the milk, half and half, eggs, melted butter, and vanilla.

Heat a large skillet over medium heat, and add a bit of butter as needed to prevent sticking. Place 1 or 2 slices of brioche into the egg mixture, turning gently to coat both sides. Do not let the pieces soak: Brioche is delicate and will fall apart. Add the slices to the skillet, and cook until they are brown on both sides, about 3 minutes per side.

Transfer the cooked pieces back to the baking sheet, and keep them warm in the oven. Repeat with the remaining pieces.

If using the jam, whisk it to thin it a little, and add it to the sliced strawberries, to glaze.

To serve, place two pieces of French toast together, bottom side to bottom side, creating the butterfly shape. If desired, spoon a small strip of Mock Clotted Cream down the center, and decorate with strawberries. A few larger pieces of strawberry can be used to "lift" the wings by placing them underneath the brioche slices. If you are not using the Mock Clotted Cream, simply decorate the center of each butterfly toast with strawberries, and serve. The glazed berries make a delicious syrup, but feel free to serve with your favorite maple syrup as well.

WHO'S GOT THE RICE CRISPY BUTTONS?

 Yield: About 12 buttons   **Gluten Free**

One of Wonderland's most popular games is "Button, Button, Who's Got the Button?" This playful recipe pays homage to Tweedledum and Tweedledee's beloved pastime. But beware—the game will be short lived when players get a taste of these delightful rice treats. After all, when traveling through Tulgey Wood, it *is* rather common to lose something . . .

6 cups puffed rice cereal

½ cup pulverized freeze-dried blueberries

10 ounces marshmallows

1 tablespoon unsalted butter

Purple sanding sugar

Licorice laces (optional)

Special Tools:

Large round cookie cutters, 2½ and 1½ inches in diameter

Stiff plastic or metal straw

Prepare an 11-by-14-inch casserole dish by lining it with parchment paper. In a large bowl, mix the rice cereal and the pulverized blueberries.

In a heatproof microwave bowl, combine the marshmallows and the butter. Heat for 1 minute, and then stir until the butter and marshmallow are completely melted. Add the marshmallow mixture to the cereal mixture. Stir until well combined.

Press the mixture into the baking pan so that it is compact and level. Allow to set for 10 to 15 minutes.

Using the 2½-inch cookie cutter, cut out as many circles as you can. Use the smaller cookie cutter to press a deep groove into each circle. In the center of the inner circle, use the straw to make three button holes.

Sprinkle each treat with purple sanding sugar. Store in an airtight container until serving, with layers of parchment in between the treats. When ready to serve, "lace" the treats with licorice, if using, by running the licorice laces through the three button holes.

CHAPTER FIVE

A Mad Tea Party

Venturing further into the forest, one may stumble upon a most unusual setup. Setting the stage for the Mad Hatter's tea party is a long, rectangular table framed by mismatched chairs and set with a peculiar collection of crockery. Here, among tilted teacups and crooked cakes, the Mad Hatter, the March Hare, and the Dormouse enjoy their Unbirthday Party. And an adventurous gastronome might discover some of Wonderland's *finest* treats here—each one best served with tea and, of course, polite conversation. Move down, move down!

HE WENT *THAT* WAY TEA SANDWICHES

 Yield: About 12 sandwiches of each type

When hosting a tea party, one should always offer a tray of light bites. From egg salad teacups to hibiscus cucumber hearts and buttons of smoked salmon and chive, these flavorful sandwiches pair well with both black and herbal teas. Just be sure to use the *very* best butter—the Mad Hatter does, after all.

EGG SALAD TEACUPS

 Gluten Free*, Vegetarian

¼ cup white balsamic vinegar

1 Earl Grey tea bag

6 eggs, hard boiled, divided

About ¾ cup crème fraîche, divided

½ teaspoon kosher salt

24 pieces soft sandwich bread, such as wheat, white, or buttermilk

About 2 cups micro arugula leaves

Special Tools:

3-inch-tall teacup cookie cutter or 3-inch-diameter biscuit cutter

> **Notes:** Leftover crusts and bread scraps can be saved and turned into bread crumbs or croutons for use in other recipes.
>
> This recipe can easily be adapted to gluten-free diets if made with gluten-free bread.

In a microwave-safe bowl, add the white balsamic vinegar and the contents of the tea bag. Microwave the mixture for 1 minute. Let the tea steep for at least 3 to 5 minutes.

Peel and mince five hard-boiled eggs, and place them into a medium bowl. Refrigerate the sixth egg until needed, for garnish. Stir ½ cup crème fraîche, the tea-vinegar mixture, and salt into the eggs, and thoroughly combine. Egg salad can be made a day ahead, stored in an airtight container, and refrigerated.

Use the cookie cutter to cut out two teacups from the bread for each sandwich, leaving the crust on the bottom edge for the base of the cup.

Spread a very light layer of crème fraîche (about ½ teaspoon) on one side of each teacup. Put a tablespoon of egg filling in the middle of half the teacups, leaving the side edges free. Sprinkle arugula leaves, and place another bread piece on top, creamed side to creamed side, pressing the edges together with a fork or your fingers. Leave the top of the teacup open, to form a pocket. If serving immediately, proceed to step 5; otherwise, refrigerate, covered, for up to 3 hours. Garnish when ready to serve.

When ready to garnish, slice the last egg crosswise, and then slice each piece in half. Garnish each teacup pocket with an egg slice as if it were a lemon wedge.

Continued on page 94

Continued from page 93

SMOKED SALMON AND CHIVE BUTTONS

 Gluten Free

4 ounces cold smoked salmon

1½ cups whipped cream cheese

3 tablespoons snipped chives, plus 12 stems for garnish

1 tablespoon white balsamic vinegar

Freshly ground black pepper

24 pieces dark rye or black bread

3- or 4-inch biscuit cutter

Roughly chop the smoked salmon, and add it to a medium bowl. Add the cream cheese, chives, vinegar, and black pepper (to taste). Stir to thoroughly combine.

Use a 3- or 4-inch biscuit cutter (whatever fills out the bread slices best) to cut 24 circles. Use a metal straw to "cut" two button holes from half the bread circles, and lace the holes with one chive stem each.

Divide the spread among the remaining twelve circles, and top with a laced bread button, pressing gently to seal. Serve immediately, or refrigerate covered for up to 3 hours.

Notes: Leftover crusts and bread scraps can be saved and turned into bread crumbs or croutons for use in other recipes.

This recipe can easily be adapted to gluten-free diets if made with gluten-free bread.

HIBISCUS CUCUMBER HEARTS

 Gluten Free*, Vegetarian

1½ cups boiling water

1½ teaspoons salt

1½ tablespoons white balsamic vinegar

4 hibiscus tea bags

2 English cucumbers, peeled

½ cup unsalted butter, softened

1 tablespoon finely chopped fresh dill

¼ teaspoon freshly ground black pepper (or to taste)

6 pieces white bread

About a 3-inch heart cookie cutter

> **Note:** This recipe can easily be adapted to gluten-free diets if made with gluten-free bread.

Combine the water, salt, vinegar, and tea bags in a large heatproof bowl or measuring cup, and allow to steep for 5 minutes. Remove the tea bags, and discard.

Use a vegetable peeler to create wide ribbons of cucumber until you reach the seed core. Add the ribbons of cucumber to the tea mixture. Cover and refrigerate the tea mixture, and allow it to quick-pickle at least 30 minutes and up to 1 hour. Discard any remaining cucumber or reserve for another use.

Combine the butter, dill, and freshly ground black pepper. Set aside until needed.

When ready to assemble, drain the cucumber ribbons and pat dry. Spread a thin layer of filling, edge to edge, on each piece of bread. Cover each piece of bread with cucumber ribbons, overlapping slightly for full coverage. Repeat with all six pieces of bread.

Place the heart cookie cutter close to the edge of a sandwich, and use a paring knife to cut around the cookie cutter. Repeat, cutting two hearts per sandwich. Serve immediately, or refrigerate, covered, for up to 3 hours.

CURIOSI-TEA

 Yield: About 8 cups, or about 12 servings over ice   **Gluten Free, Vegetarian, Vegan**

From England to Wonderland, it is widely accepted that no party is complete without a proper spot of tea. Sweet, familiar, and thoroughly chilled, this iced variety can be served at any celebration. After all, it is generally known that the best way to offer one's congratulations is with another cup of tea!

1 cup canned lychee in syrup
8 cups water
6 Jasmine green tea bags
Zest of 1 lemon
Juice of 1 lemon (optional)

Purée the lychees (along with their syrup) in a food processor or blender, and strain the purée through a fine mesh strainer. Set aside.

In a medium pot, boil the water, remove from heat, and steep the tea bags for 3 to 5 minutes. Remove the tea bags, and transfer the tea to a large pitcher. Add the lychee and the lemon zest. Taste the tea; if you would like it a little less sweet, add the lemon juice, to taste. Chill until serving. Serve over ice.

Teacup Treasures with Shrimp Salad

 Yield: About 6 servings

Wonderland offers up surprises around every corner—a talking doorknob, an inquisitive caterpillar, and one *very* peculiar tea party. This savory, teacup-shape pastry fits right in with the Mad Hatter's eccentric world. Light and filled with a refreshing shrimp salad, the Pâte à Choux Teacup embodies the frivolous spirit of the Mad Tea Party while simultaneously offering up a protein-rich snack. Clean cup, clean cup!

Shrimp Salad:

1 English cucumber, peeled, seeded, and diced
1 pound bay shrimp (fresh or frozen)
¼ cup crème fraîche
¼ cup chopped fresh parsley
1 tablespoon finely chopped fresh dill
1 tablespoon minced garlic
1 tablespoon capers, drained
3 tablespoons lemon juice (or juice of 1 lemon)
2 tablespoons seasoned rice vinegar
½ teaspoon salt
Freshly ground black pepper

Pâte à Choux Teacup:

1 cup whole milk
½ cup unsalted butter, cut into 1-tablespoon chunks
½ teaspoon salt
1 cup all-purpose flour
4 eggs, at room temperature

To assemble:

6 slices of lemon, for serving

Special Tools:

Pastry bag
3-inch silicone sphere mold

To make the shrimp salad: Place the cucumber pieces in a colander placed inside a bowl, and allow them to drain while you are prepping the shrimp and the remaining ingredients for the dressing.

If you are using frozen shrimp, thaw according to the package directions, and place them in a large bowl. If you are using fresh shrimp, pat them dry and place them in a large bowl.

In a small bowl, mix the crème fraîche, parsley, dill, garlic, capers, lemon juice, and rice vinegar for the dressing.

Add the drained cucumber to the shrimp. Toss the shrimp and cucumber with the dressing, and season with salt and black pepper (to taste). Refrigerate until needed.

Continued on page 99

Continued from page 97

To make the Pâte à Choux Teacups: Preheat the oven to 400°F, and line two baking sheets with a baking mat or parchment paper.

In a large saucepan over medium-high heat, combine the milk, butter, and salt. Bring to a boil, and add the flour. Stir vigorously with a wooden spoon until the mixture is smooth and is not sticking to the spoon or the pot. If the mixture looks rough or butter leaks out, just keep stirring until it comes together. When the mixture is smooth and formed into dough, remove it from the heat and transfer it to a bowl.

Allow the mixture to cool for 5 minutes. Begin adding the eggs one at a time. Beat after each egg until the egg is completely incorporated and the mixture is smooth again.

Place the dough into a disposable pastry bag, and snip a ¼-inch tip off the end. On one of the lined baking sheets, pipe six 3-inch handles, giving one end a strong hook. This will hang from the rim of your cup.

Place the sphere mold on the other baking sheet, and snip another ¼ inch off the end of the pastry bag. Pipe dough around each mold, starting about ½ inch from the bottom and piping all the way around, working your way to the top. Build rows of dough like a beehive. With a damp finger, gently smooth the top of the dough. This will become the bottom of your teacup.

Bake for 10 minutes, and then turn the oven down to 350°F. Bake for another 5 minutes, and check the handles. Remove the handles when they are brown, dry, and crisp to the touch. Allow them to cool on a wire rack.

Continue to bake the cups another 20 to 25 minutes until they are brown and are dry and crisp to the touch. Remove from the oven, and allow to cool for 2 or 3 minutes before gently removing them from the molds and placing them upright on the baking sheet. Allow the teacups to dry in the cooling oven.

To assemble: Place each teacup on a tea saucer, and fill with a generous ½ cup of shrimp salad. Place a handle on the edge of each cup, and garnish with a slice of lemon. Serve immediately.

DORMOUSE MACARONS

 Yield: About 20 macarons   **Gluten Free, Vegetarian**

In Wonderland, it is common knowledge that if you can't think, you shouldn't talk. And while one needn't think about whether to serve these delightful jam-filled cookies, one will certainly have *loads* to talk about when they appear at the table! Sweet, soft, and with the slightest hint of crunch, these macarons are the hit of any tea party. And they *do* make a rather delectable unbirthday present . . .

⅔ cup slivered, blanched almonds

1 cup powdered sugar

2 egg whites, at room temperature

¼ cup granulated sugar

Pink or red food coloring

¼ teaspoon rose water

½ cup raspberry jam

Luster dust (optional)

Special Tools:

Pastry bag fitted with a ½-inch-round pastry tip

> **Note:** These are best if made 1 to 2 days ahead. This allows the center to soften slightly, creating the perfect macaron texture: crisp on the outside and soft on the inside.

Lower the oven racks to the lower third of the oven, and preheat to 350°F. Line two baking sheets with parchment paper.

In the bowl of a food processor fitted with a blade attachment, process the almonds for 1 minute. Add the powdered sugar, and process 1 minute more.

Use a fine mesh strainer over a mixing bowl, and pass the almond mixture through the strainer by pushing it through with a stiff spatula. Transfer any remaining solids back to the food processor, and process again for another minute. Transfer the mixture back to the strainer, and repeat the process until 2 tablespoons or less of the solids remain. Discard the solids, and set aside the almond mixture.

In the bowl of a stand mixer fitted with a whisk attachment, gently mix the egg whites and granulated sugar on low until just combined. Raise the speed to medium-high, and beat for 2 minutes; then raise the speed to high, and beat 2 minutes more or until the mixture is glossy and holds stiff peaks.

Add the food coloring to achieve the desired hue, add the rose water, and beat for another 30 seconds.

Remove the bowl from the stand mixer, and add the almond mixture all at once. Use a spatula to pull the almond mixture through the egg whites, pressing against the sides of the bowl with each stroke. Repeat until the mixture flows like a thick batter. Do not overwork, or the macarons will not hold their shape.

Fill the pastry bag with the batter, and use a small dot to adhere the parchment to the cookie sheet at all four corners. With the tip about ½ inch off the surface of the baking sheet, pipe the batter into a ¾-inch round, spacing the rounds 1 inch apart. Tap each baking sheet several times on the counter, to release any air bubbles.

Bake for 13 to 15 minutes, rotating the sheets halfway through, until risen and just set. Allow the cookies to cool completely on the baking sheet.

Spread or pipe a thin layer of jam on the flat side of half the rounds, and top with the second half of the rounds. If decorating with luster dust, it can be either brushed on dry or mixed with a small amount of vodka and then painted on in designs. Store the cookies refrigerated in an airtight container between layers of parchment for up to 3 days.

POCKET WATCH POPPYSEED SCONES WITH MOCK CLOTTED CREAM

✿ **Yield:** About 6 scones and about 2 cups Mock Clotted Cream   **Scones:** Vegetarian, **Cream:** Gluten Free, Vegetarian

There's only one way to stop a mad watch, a fact the dear White Rabbit learns rather abruptly. But there are multitudes of ways to prepare a proper British scone. Of course, the finest bakers fill their scones with copious amounts of the best butter and a healthy dollop of flavored jam . . . or even that beloved English delicacy, clotted cream. The traditional version of Alice's rich Devonshire cream requires a laborious process of heating, cooling, and skimming, but the quick-and-easy Mock Clotted Cream can be whipped up in mere minutes, allowing a chef to focus on other, more pressing matters. After all, it takes a goodly amount of work to repair a pocket watch—especially one with wheels inside!

Mock Clotted Cream:

8 ounces cream cheese, softened

1 cup heavy whipping cream

1 tablespoon granulated sugar

Scones:

2 cups all-purpose flour

⅓ cup granulated sugar

1 tablespoon baking powder

½ teaspoon salt

2 tablespoons poppy seeds, plus more for garnish

6 tablespoons unsalted butter, very cold

6 to 8 tablespoons heavy whipping cream

¼ cup plain Greek yogurt

1 egg

Gold sanding sugar

"I'm in a Jam" Homemade Strawberry-Lemon Jam (page 105) or your own favorite jam, for serving

Special Tools:

3-inch-round cookie or biscuit cutter

To make the Mock Clotted Cream: In a large bowl or the bowl of a stand mixer, beat the cream cheese until it is light and fluffy. Add in the cream, and beat slowly at first to incorporate; then turn up to high and continue to beat until the cream is light, fluffy, and smooth, 1 to 2 minutes. Add the sugar, and beat again to combine. Store in an airtight container in the refrigerator for up to 1 week.

To make the scones: Line a baking sheet with a silicone mat or parchment paper. Preheat the oven to 425°F.

In a large mixing bowl, combine the flour, sugar, baking powder, salt, and poppy seeds, and mix thoroughly.

Continued on page 104

Continued from page 103

With a pastry cutter or two knives, cut the butter into the dry ingredients until all the butter pieces are pea size or smaller.

In a small measuring cup, combine 4 tablespoons of cream with the Greek yogurt, and whisk to combine. Add the egg, and whisk again. Add this mixture to the flour mixture, and stir to combine. Keep the measuring cup nearby. To bring the dough together, gently knead it with your hands to incorporate any remaining dry ingredients; you might need to add another tablespoon of cream.

Turn out the dough onto the prepared baking sheet, and gently form it into a circle about 8 inches across and about 1 inch thick. Use the cookie cutter to cut out as many scones as possible. Use some of the scraps to create the pocket watch–shaped "fob" at the top, and place this under the round, pressing gently to adhere. Gather up the remaining scraps, and press them back together, keeping the dough about an inch thick; cut out more scones, and use the new scraps to create more "fobs."

Add an additional tablespoon of cream to the measuring cup, stir, and use a pastry brush to wash the top of each scone. Sprinkle the round watch parts with the gold sanding sugar, and sprinkle the fobs with more poppy seeds.

Bake the scones for 12 to 15 minutes until they are golden brown. Allow them to cool for 10 minutes, and serve with Mock Clotted Cream and jam.

When completely cool, leftover scones can be stored in an airtight container for 2 to 3 days.

"I'M IN A JAM" HOMEMADE STRAWBERRY-LEMON JAM

 Yield: About four 8-ounce jars   **Gluten Free, Vegetarian, Vegan**

Sitting down at a table without being invited is *very* rude. But one shall never lack for invitations after mastering this timeless recipe. Homemade jam is a British staple that's long been served at all the best tea parties. This version offers a particularly inspired pairing: Sweet berries and zesty lemon come together in a delightfully tangy spread. Simply pop a spot into a pot—or upon the nose of a dormouse!

Juice and zest of 1 lemon

4 cups (about 1 pound) chopped strawberries

3 cups granulated sugar, divided

Special Tools:

4 clean 8-ounce jam jars with tight-fitting lids

Remove the zest, without pith, from one lemon. Finely dice the lemon zest, and add it with the strawberries, 1 cup of the sugar, and the lemon juice to an airtight container; stir to combine. Let the mixture macerate at room temperature for 1 hour.

Transfer the strawberry sugar mixture to a large saucepan, and bring to a rolling boil over high heat. Reduce to medium, stirring frequently, and keep at a low boil for 15 to 20 minutes or until a quick set test shows gelling (see note).

Remove the mixture from heat, ladle into four clean jars, and seal with tight-fitting lids. Allow the jam to cool for about 30 minutes, and then refrigerate until serving. The jam can be stored in the refrigerator for 1 month or frozen for 6 months. Jam makes a great gift; just be sure to label it appropriately: "Keep refrigerated for up to 1 month."

> **Notes:** This is best made at least 1 day ahead of serving so that it can continue to set and the flavor can meld.
>
> A quick set test: Before you start to cook the jam, place a small plate in the freezer. After cooking the jam for at least 15 minutes, remove the plate from the freezer and put about a tablespoon of jam on it. When the plate is tilted, the jam should move only slowly, or barely at all. If it still runs quickly, pop the plate back into the freezer, continue to cook the jam for another 5 minutes, and check again.
>
> Are you an experienced canner? Feel free to use your favorite canning method to can this instead of refrigerating.

UNBIRTHDAY PAR-TEA CUPCAKES

 Yield: 24 servings   **Vegetarian**

It's dreadfully disappointing that, in any given year, one will have but a *single* birthday to celebrate. Thankfully, there also happen to be 364 *unbirthdays* to observe! And as everyone knows, the best way to celebrate a birthday—un- or otherwise—is with a cake. Best served with tea (no dormouse required), these Unbirthday Par-tea Cupcakes are a distinctively delectable delicacy. The Mad Hatter and the March Hare enjoy a multitiered confection that quite literally explodes with flavor. But if one is cooking for a smaller group, or if one prefers the baked goods to be served fuss free, this particular version is most delightful. Either way, do be sure to follow the instructions. After all, curiosity often leads to trouble . . .

Edible Candles:

1½ cups white chocolate chips

¼ cup corn syrup

Food coloring in pale yellow, pink, and green

Up to 1 cup powdered sugar

24 (about 2 tablespoons) slivered almonds

¼ teaspoon peppermint oil (optional)

Cherry Filling:

10 ounces pitted cherries (fresh or frozen)

½ cup granulated sugar

Juice of 1 lemon

¼ teaspoon xanthan gum

¼ teaspoon clove

Lemon Curd:

3 large eggs

½ cup granulated sugar

Zest from 2 lemons

½ cup fresh strained lemon juice

6 tablespoons unsalted butter, cut into small pieces

1 teaspoon blue spirulina (optional)

To make the edible candles: In a microwave-safe bowl, melt the chocolate by microwaving 30 seconds at a time and stirring between each addition.

When the chocolate is completely melted, add in the corn syrup; stir thoroughly to combine. The mixture might have a slightly curdled texture at this point.

Split the mixture into three bowls. To each bowl, add 1 to 2 drops of food coloring at a time, stirring, until the desired shade is reached. Wrap each bowl in plastic wrap, and let the contents stand at room temperature for 2 to 3 hours or overnight.

When ready to use, dust a work surface with the powdered sugar, and knead each color of modeling chocolate until it is smooth and elastic. Add more powdered sugar as needed, to keep the chocolate from sticking.

Shape candles, either straight or into a twist, about 3 inches long. Insert a slivered almond into one end, and brush the almond with peppermint oil, if using. Place the candles on a baking sheet lined with a baking mat or parchment paper. Allow them to set in the refrigerator for 30 minutes. Transfer the candles to an airtight container, separated by parchment until needed. Use any extra modeling chocolate to make small leaves, flowers, or other decorations, as desired.

To make the cherry filling: In a medium pot over medium heat, add the cherries, sugar, and lemon juice. Bring to a simmer until the sugar is completely dissolved. Use the back of a spoon to smash most of the cherries. Add the xanthan gum and clove, and simmer for about 2 minutes or until slightly thickened. Remove to a heatproof container with a lid, cover, and refrigerate until needed.

Continued on page 108

Continued from page 107

Vanilla Cake Base:

2¼ cups all-purpose flour

1 teaspoon baking powder

½ teaspoon baking soda

½ teaspoon salt

4 tablespoons (½ stick) salted butter, softened

1 cup granulated sugar

4 ounces sour cream

2 eggs

¾ cup whole milk

1 tablespoon vanilla bean paste

Buttercream:

1½ cups pasteurized egg whites

3 cups granulated sugar

2 pounds (8 sticks) salted butter, softened, cut into 1-tablespoon chunks

2 teaspoons vanilla

Chocolate Ganache Filling:

8 ounces ruby chocolate (or semisweet chocolate), chopped into small pieces

¾ cup heavy whipping cream

To assemble:

24 teacups, one for each cupcake

Chocolate pearls (optional)

White chocolate pearls (optional)

¾ cup heavy whipping cream

To make the lemon curd: In a medium nonreactive saucepan, whisk together the eggs and sugar until the mixture is light in color.

Add the lemon zest and lemon juice, and whisk to combine. Put the saucepan over medium heat, whisking constantly, and add the butter a piece at a time until it is melted and completely incorporated. Be sure to scrape the corners of the pan. Continue to simmer for a few seconds or until the mixture is thickened. Do not overcook.

Remove the mixture from heat, and scrape it through a mesh strainer into a container with a tight-fitting lid.

Stir in the blue spirulina, if using, and refrigerate until needed.

To make the vanilla cake: Preheat the oven to 350°F, and thoroughly grease a 12-capacity muffin pan.

In a medium bowl, whisk together the flour, baking powder, baking soda, and salt, and set aside.

In the bowl of a stand mixer fitted with a paddle attachment, beat together the butter, sugar, and sour cream until the mixture is pale and fluffy. Add the eggs one at a time, beating after each addition until combined.

Add in the flour mixture in two batches, alternating with the milk. Stir to combine after each addition. Add the vanilla bean paste, and stir to incorporate.

Fill each muffin cup two-thirds full with batter. Bake for 20 to 25 minutes or until a cake tester comes out clean. Allow the cupcakes to cool on a wire rack for 15 minutes before gently removing them from the muffin pan; cool completely.

To make the chocolate cake variation: Increase the sugar in the cake ingredients to 1½ cups. Combine ¾ cup of unsweetened cocoa powder with 1 cup hot water to replace the milk, and replace the vanilla paste with vanilla extract or strong coffee. Proceed with steps 11 through 15.

To make the buttercream: Place a heatproof measuring cup or bowl inside a saucepan. Fill the saucepan with water until the water level reaches halfway up the cup. Remove the measuring cup, and turn the heat to medium. Bring the water to a simmer.

In the measuring cup, combine the egg whites with the sugar, and whisk until blended. Place the measuring cup into the simmering water, and cook, stirring constantly, until the sugar is completely dissolved and the mixture is hot.

With an oven mitt, carefully remove the measuring cup containing the sugar-egg mixture from the saucepan, and transfer the mixture to the bowl of a stand mixer fitted with a whisk attachment. Whisk the egg-sugar mixture on high until it is completely cool, up to 7 to 10 minutes. The mixture should be opaque and white, with elastic ribbons flowing from the beater—a loose, sticky meringue. This could take 7 to 10 minutes.

Add the softened butter to the meringue one piece at a time, with the mixer on low, until all the butter is incorporated.

Add the vanilla, turn up the mixer speed to medium, and mix until smooth, 1 to 2 minutes more. Set aside.

To make the chocolate ganache filling: In a microwave-safe bowl, cover the chocolate with the cream, and microwave for 1 minute. Allow the filling to stand for 5 minutes, and then stir until smooth.

To assemble the cake: Slice each cupcake in half horizontally to separate the top from the bottom. Add a small dollop of buttercream to the bottom of each teacup, and place the bottom half of a cupcake on it.

Choose a filling (cherry filling, lemon curd, or chocolate ganache), and spoon 2 to 3 tablespoons of it onto the bottom of the cupcake. It is okay if the filling spills over into the cup.

Top with a matching cupcake top, and frost the top with buttercream. If making a chocolate variation, use the chocolate pearls to keep track of the vanilla and chocolate cakes. Use the candle colors to keep track of the fillings.

When ready to serve, light the almonds as you would a candle.

CHAPTER SIX

The Red Queen's Kingdom

The deepest corner of Wonderland is also its darkest. It might be lined with verdant foliage and vibrant rose bushes, but behind the cheerful appearance of the Royal Garden rests a villainous vibration. The Red Queen manages her kingdom with a consistently unpredictable rage that holds her subjects in a constant state of concern. One can only imagine that the Queen's cuisine must be prepared with the utmost care and tested under extremely stringent standards. After all, it would never do to put a foot out of turn—not when heads are on the line!

TOAST SOLDIERS WITH CODDLED EGGS

 Yield: 2 servings **Gluten Free*, Vegetarian***

In food and in life, nothing should ever be *too* serious. This dish perfectly pairs Britain's national sense of duty with Alice's youthful air of adventure. Much like the Queen's Guard protects the palace, these toasted sentinels look after their coddled companions. Make way for the Toast Soldiers!

Special Tools:

2 egg coddlers or low wide-mouth mason jars

Large saucepan with tight-fitting lid and rack or folded tea towel

2 teaspoons salted butter, divided, plus more as desired

1 slice prosciutto, diced, divided

2 teaspoons shredded Parmesan cheese, divided

2 large eggs

1 tablespoon snipped chives, divided (see note)

Freshly ground black pepper

2 pieces sliced bread

Notes: Use kitchen shears to snip the chives. Chives bruise easily, so unless you're highly skilled with a kitchen knife, we highly recommend using kitchen shears to snip the chives into pieces.

This recipe can easily be adapted to gluten-free diets if made with gluten-free bread and vegetarian diets if made without prosciutto.

Place the rack or folded tea towel inside the saucepan, and add the two empty coddlers or jars inside. Fill the pan with water until it reaches the bottom of the coddler lids. Remove the jars from the saucepan, and bring the water to a boil over medium-high heat.

While the water is boiling, use ½ teaspoon of butter on each coddler, to thoroughly grease it. Split the prosciutto and Parmesan cheese between the bottoms of each coddler. Crack the eggs, and gently add one to each coddler. Top with an additional ½ teaspoon of butter each and ½ tablespoon of chives each. Add freshly ground black pepper, to taste.

Tightly seal each coddler or jar. When the water reaches a boil, place the coddlers or jars inside the pot. Cover immediately, and reduce heat to simmer. Simmer 8 to 10 minutes or until eggs are set to desired firmness. Using tongs or oven mitts, gently remove the eggs from the pot.

For the soldiers, butter both sides of each slice of bread, and place the slices in a hot skillet or on a hot griddle, to toast each side to the desired doneness. Remove all crusts except for the top crust, and slice into rectangular "soldiers."

To serve, place each coddler on a small plate, with the soldiers alongside.

PAINTING THE ROSES RED PAVLOVA

 Yield: 8 servings   **Gluten Free, Vegetarian**

The Queen's garden is dotted with delicate roses and tidily trimmed topiaries. And what better dish with which to pay homage to the gracefully growing flora than one named for a brilliant ballerina? In this pavlova, light meringue provides a supportive base for a bushel of beautiful berries. Just be sure to choose the *red* kind!

Raspberry Sauce:

10 ounces frozen raspberries (or fresh, if available)
1 cup sparkling apple cider
1 cup granulated sugar
1 teaspoon freshly ground black pepper

Meringue:

¼ cup meringue powder
½ cup room-temperature water
1 cup superfine sugar
1 teaspoon vanilla

Whipped Cream:

1 cup heavy cream
1 tablespoon powdered sugar
1 teaspoon vanilla

Special Tools:

1 parchment-lined cookie sheet
Pastry bag fitted with a large star tip

To make the raspberry sauce: In a medium saucepan over medium heat, add the raspberries, apple cider, sugar, and black pepper. Stir to combine and dissolve the sugar. Bring to a boil, and then reduce to a simmer. Simmer for 15 to 20 minutes or until the sauce begins to coat the back of the spoon.

Remove the mixture from heat, and allow to cool 5 to 10 minutes before straining it through a fine mesh strainer to remove any seeds. Be sure to scrape the bottom of the strainer and incorporate the jammy substance. Store the sauce in an airtight container, and refrigerate until needed.

To make the meringue: Preheat the oven to 250°F. Line a baking sheet with parchment paper.

Trace eight 4-inch circles on the parchment paper.

In the bowl of a stand mixer fitted with a whisk attachment, add the meringue powder and water. Whip on high speed until soft peaks form.

With the mixer running on low, gradually add the sugar, and mix until incorporated, scraping the bowl as needed. Raise the speed to medium and continue to whip until stiff peaks form. Add the vanilla, and whisk again to combine.

Fill the pastry bag with the meringue. Using the circles as a guide, pipe a large rosette, starting at the center and working out. Pipe a small rosette on top of the first one. Repeat until you have piped all the rosettes.

Bake for 20 to 23 minutes, or until crisp and dry on the outside. Pavlovas will continue to crisp as they cool. Allow the pavlova to cool completely on the baking sheet.

Fill a whipped cream canister with 1 cup of heavy cream, 1 tablespoon of powdered sugar, and 1 teaspoon of vanilla. Pipe a large rosette of whipped cream on each dessert plate, top with a meringue, and serve with a small glass or bowl of the raspberry sauce. Let the guests "paint" their own pavlova.

> **Notes:** If a whipped cream canister is not available, whip the cream with a mixer and put it in a piping bag fitted with a large star tip.
>
> Meringue powder contains egg, so it is not vegan.

HER ROYAL MAJESTY'S CROWN ROAST

Yield: 10 to 12 servings **Gluten Free**

Heavy is the head that wears the crown. But what of those who eat it? With savory onions and sweet apple slices, this pork crown roast will be the hit of *any* dinner party—and will certainly leave guests curtseying to their chef! Just remember that, when serving royalty, presentation always matters: Make sure the spokes of the crown are perfectly situated. After all, one wouldn't want to anger the Red Queen . . .

1 trimmed and tied pork crown roast (see note)

2 tablespoons fresh rosemary leaves, minced

4 tablespoons fresh thyme leaves, minced

¼ cup loosely packed fresh sage leaves, minced

2 teaspoons red chili flakes

2 teaspoons salt

¼ cup olive oil

1 apple, cored and sliced

1 yellow onion, quartered and then quartered again

¼ cup apple cider vinegar

½ cup sweet vermouth

1 tablespoon unsalted butter

One hour before cooking, place the pork in a large roasting pan; let it stand at room temperature. Mix the rosemary, thyme, sage, chili flakes, salt, and olive oil in a small bowl, and rub the mixture all over the roast.

Toss the apple and onion with the vinegar, and pour all the liquid into the center cavity of the roast.

Lower the oven rack to the lower third of the oven, making sure that there is enough clearance for the crown; you might need to remove a rack. Preheat the oven to 400°F.

Cook the roast for 20 minutes, and then lower the oven temperature to 250°F. Cook for 15 to 18 minutes per pound or until a meat thermometer reaches 160°F.

Tent the pork with foil, and let it rest for 15 to 20 minutes. The temperature will continue to rise while it rests. Carefully transfer the roast to a large serving platter.

Put the roasting pan on the stove (over two burners, if possible), and deglaze with the sweet vermouth. Add the butter, and stir to melt and combine. Transfer the liquid to a gravy boat or bowl, and serve with the roast.

> **Note:** A crown rack of pork is a large and dramatic centerpiece to any meal. It serves a crowd, so it is worth the price. In most cases, you will need to special order a crown rack. Check with your local butcher, and allow plenty of time for ordering before you need to cook it.

THE QUEEN'S WAY SPICED CIDER

 Yield: 6 to 8 servings   **Gluten Free, Vegetarian**

Wonderland's monarch certainly has a spicy side. The Red Queen is prone to losing her temper at the drop of a croquet ball and then blaming her opponent for driving her into such a fit. This spiced apple beverage blends cranberry, apple, and white grape juices in a brew designed to invoke the peppery personality who must *always* win at royal matches. It's a truly fitting beverage for a particularly prickly queen!

4 cups unsweetened cranberry juice
4 cups unfiltered apple cider
2 cups white grape juice
½ cup honey
1 cinnamon stick, broken up
1 teaspoon whole peppercorns
½ teaspoon whole clove

Special Tools:
Large tea or soup infuser

Add cranberry juice, apple cider, grape juice, and honey to a large sauce pot. Add the cinnamon, peppercorns, and clove to the infuser, and lower the infuser into the pot, making sure it is submerged. Bring to a simmer, stirring to dissolve the honey, and simmer for 15 to 20 minutes.

Remove the pot from the heat, and allow the liquid to steep for 1 to 2 hours. After 1 hour, you can taste-test the spice level. After steeping, remove the infuser, and refrigerate until serving.

To serve, reheat in a pot or mug in the microwave. This can also be served over ice.

> **Wonderland Tip:**
> If you don't have an infuser large enough to hold the spices, add them straight to the pot. When the mixture is cool, strain it through a fine mesh strainer into a storage container.

PLAYING CARD STRATA

 Yield: 8 to 10 servings  **Vegetarian**

The Queen's tightly wound gardeners frequently find that they must reshuffle their plans. After all, flowers don't always grow the way one wants them to! This layered casserole serves as a savory nod to those hardworking cards and the many varietals of roses they cultivate—naturally, or otherwise.

About 1 tablespoon salted butter, for greasing the pan

5 slices white bread, with the crusts removed

5 slices dark rye or black bread, with the crusts removed, plus 1 more slice for garnish

2 cups (about 4 ounces) shredded Gruyère cheese

½ cup (about 2 ounces) grated Parmesan cheese

4 scallions, thinly sliced, white to light green

¼ cup finely chopped parsley leaves

¼ cup sundried tomatoes, drained and finely chopped, plus 8 more whole sundried tomatoes, for garnish

8 eggs

1½ cups milk

1½ cups half and half

½ teaspoon salt

Freshly ground black pepper

Special Tools:

Small card suit–shape cookie cutters

> **Note:** This needs to sit overnight or up to 48 hours so that the bread can absorb the custard.

Slice each piece of bread into 3-inch strips. Grease the bottom and sides of a 9-by-13-inch or 4-quart baking pan.

In a small bowl, mix the Gruyère and Parmesan cheeses. In a medium bowl, mix together the scallions, parsley, and chopped sundried tomatoes.

Layer the bottom of the pan with bread, alternating between white and rye. Scatter half the herb-tomato mixture over it. Scatter a third of the cheese over the herbs. Top with more bread, the remaining herb-tomato mixture, and another third of the cheese. Top with the third layer of bread, and sprinkle with the remaining cheese.

Using the cookie cutters, cut out clubs and spades from the extra dark rye bread slice, and cut out hearts and diamonds from the sundried tomatoes. Place the clubs and spades on every other top slice of bread, and cover the baking dish with a lid or foil. Refrigerate overnight or up to 48 hours. Put the tomato hearts and diamonds in a small airtight container, and refrigerate until needed.

In a large bowl, combine the eggs, milk, half and half, salt, and ground pepper, and whisk until throughly combined. Pour the mixture slowly over the casserole dish, allowing time for the bread to absorb part of the custard. Once all the custard mixture has been added to the pan, cover, and refrigerate overnight or up to 48 hours.

Preheat the oven to 350°F, and bake the contents of the baking dish for 30 minutes. Add the sundried tomato hearts and diamonds in the empty places, and bake an additional 10 to 15 minutes or until a knife stuck in the custard comes out clean. Allow the dish to cool 10 minutes before serving.

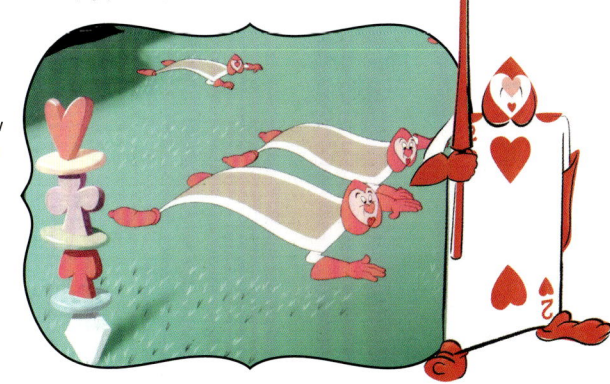

OH, MY FUR AND WHISKERS SKEWERS

 Yield: 4 sandwiches   **Gluten Free*, Vegetarian, Vegan**

The Red Queen is quick to spiral into anger. And although some might claim that she's *slightly* unhinged, it is equally possible that the rosy ruler is simply hungry! These unusual skewered sandwiches will turn any frown upside down—especially when served with a generous dollop of nut butter. Just be sure to offer the Queen her sandwich first. All ways are *her* ways, after all!

8 pieces white bread
⅓ cup pistachio butter
About ¼ cup crushed freeze-dried raspberries

Special Tools:
Parchment paper
Small 4- to 6-inch skewers

With a rolling pin, roll out each piece of bread, short end to short end. Gently remove the crusts from each piece.

Spread about 2 teaspoons of the pistachio butter onto each piece. Sprinkle about 2 teaspoons of the raspberries over the pistachio butter.

Gently roll up each piece, starting on a long side, and wrap in a piece of parchment paper, twisting the ends to close. Chill for at least 30 minutes.

Once chilled, unwrap and slice each roll into five or six slices, about ¼ inch thick; gently insert a skewer through the seam, creating a lollipop. Serve immediately.

Wonderland Tip: For a more on-the-go presentation, leave the sandwiches in the parchment wraps and serve them like wrapped candy tea sandwiches. Feel free to substitute other nut or seed butters, such as almond or sunflower.

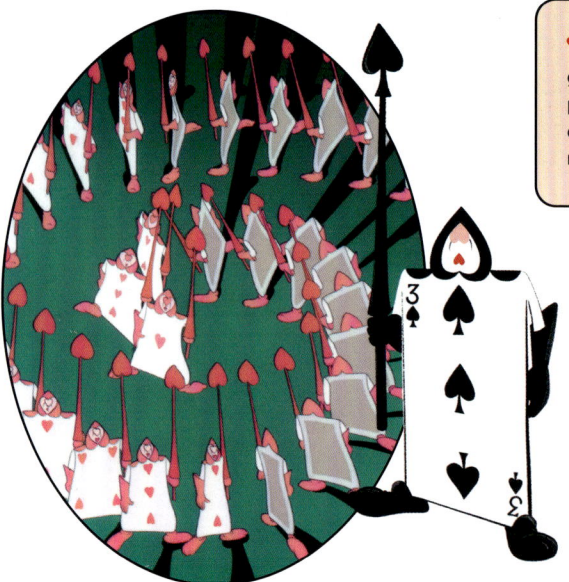

Wonderland Tip: For a more on-the-go presentation, leave the sandwiches in the parchment wraps and serve them like wrapped candy tea sandwiches. Feel free to substitute other nut or seed butters, such as almond or sunflower.

Note: This recipe can easily be adapted to gluten-free diets if made with gluten-free bread.

BITTERSWEET TRUFFLES

 Yield: About 15 truffles   **Gluten Free, Vegetarian**

The Royal Court is a study in contrasts. It is orderly yet chaotic, structured yet wild. And much like this highly sought-after delicacy, it is equal parts bitter and sweet. Any of the Queen's subjects—from the White Rabbit to the Dormouse—could appreciate this extravagant recipe, which pairs both bittersweet and milk chocolates with a hearty portion of cream. After all, one can never be truly mad while eating a truffle!

6 ounces milk chocolate, finely chopped
¼ cup heavy cream
8 ounces bittersweet chocolate
1 teaspoon crushed pink peppercorns (optional)
Corn starch, for hands

Line a baking sheet with parchment paper, and chill in the refrigerator until you are ready to form truffles.

In a heatproof bowl, cover the milk chocolate with the cream, and microwave it in 30-second bursts for 1½ minutes. Allow the mixture to sit for 5 minutes, and stir until smooth.

Cover and refrigerate for 2 to 3 hours or until stiff.

Use a melon baller to create ¾-inch balls. Coat your hands in a bit of corn starch, and roll each ball into perfect spheres. Allow the balls to come up to room temperature while you prepare the coating.

In a heatproof bowl, heat 4 ounces of the bittersweet chocolate in three 30-second bursts, stirring between each burst. Add the other 4 ounces of chocolate a little at a time, continuing to stir until all the chocolate is melted and smooth.

Use a fork or candy dipper to dip each chocolate ball into the melted chocolate, tapping to remove the excess.

Set each truffle on the chilled baking sheet, and sprinkle with a bit of pink peppercorns, if using. Chill in the refrigerator for 3 to 5 minutes, to set.

Place each truffle in a paper candy cup. Serve right away, or store in an airtight container in the refrigerator for up to 3 weeks.

VERY GOOD ADVICE GUMMIES

 Yield: About eighteen 1-inch candies

Those who live under the Queen's rule frequently find themselves in sticky situations. But not all prickly scenarios are problematic. In fact, some can be surprisingly sweet. These jelly gummy candies are every bit as fun to make as they are to eat. They're also wonderful to share with friends—as long as the Queen allows it!

One 1-ounce gelatin packet

10 tablespoons fruit juice, such as cherry, pineapple, or cranberry, divided

½ cup superfine sugar, plus more for coating finished candies

Special Tools:
Silicone candy molds

Small rimmed baking sheet

 **Note:** Gelatin is not vegan or vegetarian.

In a small bowl, whisk together the gelatin and 6 tablespoons of fruit juice, and let stand for 5 minutes.

In a small saucepan over medium-low heat, bring the remaining 4 tablespoons of fruit juice to a boil. Whisk the gelatin mixture into the saucepan until all the gelatin is dissolved.

Lower the heat, and add the sugar. Whisk until the sugar is completely dissolved. Simmer the mixture until thickened, 5 to 7 minutes.

Place the molds on the baking sheet, for easy transport. Pour the juice mixture into the silicone mold. Cool for 6 hours or overnight. Unmold the candies, and roll them in sugar to cover all sides.

Candies can be stored in the refrigerator in an airtight container, with wax paper in between the layers, until ready to serve. They can be made up to 1 week ahead.

QUEEN OF HEARTS TOMATO TART

 Yield: 6 to 8 servings   **Gluten Free, Vegetarian**

Everyone knows that the Queen of Hearts favors the color red. She simply will not tolerate deviations from her desired décor, and those who dare upset her pay a heady consequence! But even the finicky Queen would take no issue with this exquisitely lovely tomato tart. Light, sweet, and flavored with a hint of lemon, the Queen of Hearts Tomato Tart is a garden party staple and would surely be a favorite of Her Grace, Her Excellency, Her Royal Majesty, the Queen of Hearts (and the King!).

Crust:

1 cup cornmeal

1 teaspoon granulated sugar

½ teaspoon kosher salt

1 egg

2 tablespoons olive oil

½ cup finely grated sharp cheddar cheese

½ cup finely grated Parmesan cheese

Filling:

15 ounces ricotta cheese

Zest of 1 lemon

1 tablespoon finely minced parsley

1 teaspoon finely minced thyme

1 large garlic clove, minced

¼ teaspoon salt

½ teaspoon freshly ground black pepper

1 pint small red grape tomatoes

1 pint small yellow grape or cherry tomatoes

¼ teaspoon coarse finishing salt

Special Tools:

9-inch tart pan

To make the crust: Preheat the oven to 400°F.

Put the cornmeal, sugar, and salt in the bowl of a food processor fitted with a blade attachment. Process for 5 minutes, turn off the processor, and let the cornmeal mixture cool, uncovered.

Whisk the egg in a small bowl until frothy, and then whisk in the oil. Add the egg mixture and grated cheeses to the food processor with the cornmeal mixture.

Pulse the ingredients in the processor for 30 to 45 seconds until all ingredients just come together. Do not overprocess, or the crust will have a tough texture.

Press the crust mixture evenly over the bottom and up the sides of the tart pan. Bake for 14 to 16 minutes until lightly browned. Remove the crust from the oven, and allow it to cool for 15 to 20 minutes.

To make the filling: In a medium bowl, mix together the ricotta, lemon zest, parsley, thyme, garlic, salt, and black pepper. Spread the ricotta mixture in an even layer over the crust.

Slice the red grape tomatoes crosswise in half at a 45° angle, and spin one half 180° to create a heart shape. Place the red tomato sides together in stripes onto the ricotta filling, gently pressing down to hold the heart shape. Leave space between the stripes of hearts for the stripes of yellow tomatoes. Slice the yellow tomatoes in half, and place the cut side down to fill in the stripes between the tomato hearts.

Place the assembled tart back in the oven under the broiler for 5 to 10 minutes until the tomatoes are browned and the ricotta is warmed.

Remove from the oven and sprinkle with finishing salt. Allow the dish to cool before slicing and serving.

GLOSSARY

Blooming Gelatin: Blooming gelatin helps ensure that the gelatin dissolves easily and creates a smooth finished product. Using the recipe's specified amount of water and gelatin, place the water in a shallow bowl and sprinkle the gelatin evenly over the surface. Allow the gelatin to bloom for 3 to 5 minutes. You will clearly see the changes as the gelatin begins to absorb the water and swell.

Blue Spirulina: This blue-green algae grows in ponds, lakes, and alkaline waterways. Phycocyanin is a pigment derived from spirulina that gives the algae its dark blue pigment. Blue spirulina adds vibrant color to foods and drinks without compromising flavor. You can find it at heath food stores or online.

Deglaze: To deglaze is to add liquid, usually wine or stock, to a hot pan to release all the caramelized food from the pan. These caramelized bits, called fond, are full of flavor and should not be left behind. Deglazing is often the first step in making a delicious sauce.

Dutch Oven: A Dutch oven is a heavy cooking pot often made out of cast iron. It holds and distributes heat evenly, which makes it ideal for making stews or deep frying. A Dutch oven works well with high or low temperatures, so this versatile cooking tool is a handy addition to every kitchen.

Egg Wash: Whisk together one egg and 1 tablespoon of water until light and foamy. Use a pastry brush to apply the wash when the recipe requires.

Flooding Icing: This technique achieves bakery-worthy results when icing cookies. First, pipe a stiff line of icing along the edge of the cookie; then use a slightly runnier icing to fill in the outline, covering the cookies completely. Finally, use a scribe tool or a toothpick to smooth out any inconsistencies or air bubbles.

Luster Dust: This decorative material is a food-safe glitter that can be purchased online or in specialty baking departments. It can be mixed with clear alcohol to create a shimmery paint or can be brushed on dry.

Milk: The word *milk* in this book refers to dairy milk, unless otherwise specified. Any percentage of milk fat works, unless otherwise noted.

Pastry Bag, Tips, and Couplers: A pastry bag is sometimes referred to as a piping bag or a decorating bag. Available at stores that carry cake decorating supplies, these bags are cone shaped and can be either disposable or reusable. They can be used alone, by just snipping the tip of the bag at the desired size, or with piping tips. Piping tips come in a variety of designs that shape the frosting or filling as it is being extruded from the bag. Couplers fit piping tips to the outside of the pastry bag (instead of just dropping them into the bag) so that the tips can be changed out without needing to empty the bag itself.

Peeling Ginger: The easiest way to peel fresh ginger is with a small spoon: Simply use the edge of the spoon to scrape away the peel. This technique keeps the ginger root intact, creates less waste, and enables you to easily navigate all the bumps and lumps.

Salt: Feel free to use your salt of choice, unless the recipe calls for a specific kind. Kosher salt is most commonly used throughout the book.

Silicone Baking Mat: Silicone baking mats can be used with both high temperatures in the oven and subzero temperatures in the freezer. They are helpful when baking because they provide a good surface for rolling out dough and can go from prep station, to fridge or freezer, to oven without requiring you to transfer dough. Silicone mats are also extremely nonstick and easy to clean.

Vanilla Paste vs. Vanilla Extract: Vanilla bean paste delivers strong vanilla flavor and also provides beautiful vanilla bean flecks without requiring you to split and steep a vanilla bean. Vanilla paste is more expensive than vanilla extract, but in some recipes, it really shines and elevates a dish. If you don't have vanilla paste on hand, you can substitute the same amount of vanilla extract.

DIETARY CONSIDERATIONS

V = Vegetarian **V+** = Vegan
GF = Gluten-free **V*, V+** & **GF*** = Easily made vegetarian, vegan, or gluten-free with simple alterations

Chapter One: London

Lazy Daisies Garden Quiche	V		
Fairy Cake Butterflies	V		
Curiously Cornish Pasties			
The Cat's Meow Milkshake	V		
Fanciful Fish and Chips			
Perfect Pistachio Stuffed Chicken			GF
Savory Sausage Rolls			
Perfectly Potted Cheese	V		GF*

Chapter Two: Down the Rabbit Hole

Curiouser and Curiouser Chocolate-Covered Digestive Cookies	V		
Growth Potion	V		GF
Magic Cook-Keys	V		
White Rabbit Graham Cracker Cottages	V		
"I'm Really in a Stew"	V	V+	GF
Bill the Lizard's Ladder Bread	V		
White Rabbit's Garden Crudité	V		GF

Chapter Three: Ocean of Tears

An Ocean of Tears Blue Drink	V		GF
Of Cabbage Rolls and Kings			
The Sailor's Life Boat Crudité	V	V+	GF*
"Whether Pigs Have Wings" Pastries			
Caucus Race Ravioli	V		
Sun and Moon Pizza Pie			

Chapter Four: Tulgey Wood

Tweedledee & Tweedledum Brownie Cake Pops	V		
Garden Thistle Artichoke Dip	V		GF*
Cheshire Cat Panna Cotta			GF
Golden Afternoon Greens	V	V+	GF
Fanciful Fruit Shrubs	V	V+	GF
"I'm Late!" Quick Roast Vegetables	V	V+*	GF
White Rabbit's Quick Change Oats	V	V+*	GF*
Pocket Watch Cupcakes	V		
Caterpillar Crostini	V		GF*

Moroccan Chicken and Olives			GF*
A-E-I-O-Soup	V	V+*	GF*
Mushroom Perch Pie	V		
Tulgey Wood Forest Cake	V		
Forest Chutney	V	V+	GF
Crocodile Golden Scale Beets	V		GF
Bread and Butterfly Toast	V		
Who's Got the Rice Crispy Buttons?			GF

Chapter Five: A Mad Tea Party

He Went That Way Tea Sandwiches:			
Egg Salad Teacups	V		GF*
Smoked Salmon and Chive Buttons			GF*
Hibiscus Cucumber Hearts	V		GF*
Curiosi-tea	V	V+	GF
Teacup Treasures with Shrimp Salad			
Dormouse Macarons	V		GF
Pocket Watch Poppyseed Scones with Mock Clotted Cream			
Scones	V		
Mock Clotted Cream	V		GF
"I'm in a Jam" Homemade Strawberry-Lemon Jam	V	V+	GF
Unbirthday Par-Tea Cupcakes	V		

Chapter Six: The Red Queen's Kingdom

Toast Soldiers with Coddled Eggs	V*		GF*
Painting the Roses Red Pavlova	V		GF
Her Royal Majesty's Crown Roast			GF
The Queen's Way Spiced Cider	V		GF
Playing Card Strata	V		
Oh, My Fur and Whiskers Skewers	V	V+	GF*
Bittersweet Truffles	V		GF
Very Good Advice Gummies			GF
Queen of Hearts Tomato Tart	V		GF

INSIGHT EDITIONS
PO Box 3088
San Rafael, CA 94912
www.insighteditions.com

Find us on Facebook: www.facebook.com/InsightEditions
Follow us on Twitter: @insighteditions

© 2023 Disney

All rights reserved. Published by Insight Editions, San Rafael, California, in 2023.

No part of this book may be reproduced in any form without written permission from the publisher.

Gift ISBN: 979-8-88663-277-4

Publisher: Raoul Goff
VP of Licensing and Partnerships: Vanessa Lopez
VP of Creative: Chrissy Kwasnik
VP of Manufacturing: Alix Nicholaeff
VP, Editorial Director: Vicki Jaeger
Photography Direction: Judy Wiatrek Trum
Designer: Leah Bloise Lauer
Editor: Anna Wostenberg
Editorial Assistant: Grace Orriss
Managing Editor: Maria Spano
Production Editor: Katie Rokakis
Production Associate: Deena Hashem
Senior Production Manager, Subsidiary Rights: Lina s Palma Temena

Photographer: Ted Thomas
Food and Prop Stylist: Elena P. Craig
Food Styling Assistant: Patricia C. Parrish

Insight Editions, in association with Roots of Peace, will plant two trees for each tree used in the manufacturing of this book. Roots of Peace is an internationally renowned humanitarian organization dedicated to eradicating land mines worldwide and converting war-torn lands into productive farms and wildlife habitats. Roots of Peace will plant two million fruit and nut trees in Afghanistan and provide farmers there with the skills and support necessary for sustainable land use.

Manufactured in China by Insight Editions

10 9 8 7 6 5 4 3 2 1